"I can do all things through Jesus Christ who strengthens me."

Bible — Philippians 4:13

THE
VERSATILE TROPHY HUNTER

By Bill Butler

Author hunting Bighorn Sheep high in the Beartooth Mountains.

"Arise, walk about the land through its length and breadth, for I will give it to you."

Bible - Genesis 13:17

"God gives me luck in proportion to how hard I work toward achieving a goal, in proportion to how hard I try to succeed. If I make a half-hearted attempt, I really don't expect success. But if I work real hard, pull out all the stops, go for broke, try very hard from every angle I can, both physically and mentally, then I don't just hope for success, but I wholeheartedly expect it."

Bill Butler
1-19-90

DEDICATION

I dedicate this book to the memory of my mother, Helen M. Clawson Butler, may she rest in peace. I wish she could be here to read and share this with me now.

To my father, James F. Butler, who taught me many things, one of which was to hunt.

To my wife, Diana, who never stopped believing in me.

Rocky Mountain Bighorn Ram

"LIFE IS A CELEBRATION! Greet each day with enthusiasm. Live always with passion and appreciation of God's gifts to us."

Bill Butler -1991

ISBN 0-9637553-0-7

PRINTED WITH PRIDE IN THE UNITED STATES OF AMERICA

ACKNOWLEDGEMENTS

To the following people and outdoor organizations who helped to make this dream possible, I want to extend my sincere thanks and publicly acknowledge their service.

To my wife, Diana, for her patience and understanding when I am in the field, not only during hunting season, but also in the off season as well, and for her charity of invaluable assistance in the organization, design, attention to detail, and typing of this book.

Milt and Gloria Wester, of the Laurel Outlook, for their expertise in facilitating the layout of this book.

To the artists Hayden Lambson and Terry Bateman, who have such a wonderful talent, and have made this book even more special to me. Words cannot tell the two of you how much your contribution to this venture means to me and to the people who will always enjoy seeing your works. For more information on the artists please contact:

Hayden Lambson
Lambson's Wildlife Originals
1512 Ridgeway Ct.,
Pocatello, Idaho 83201
Phone (208) 233-3278

Terry Bateman
P.O. Box 371
Joliet, Montana 59041
Phone (406) 962-3273

To Mark Henckel for his encouragement and expert advice.

Walsworth Publishing for the opportunity to work with such superb professionals.

Petersen's Hunting for allowing me use of a story first published in their magazine.

Jens Selvig for his photographic know-how and undivided attention to this project.

Cover design by Eric Finstad of Advertising Design for all his ideas and craftsmanship in producing the cover.

I wish to thank these national organizations for their continued ability to inspire us to hunt, their persistent efforts to protect our hunting rights, and their continuous facility to keep us informed:

Boone & Crockett Club
Foundation for North American Wild Sheep (FNAWS)
National Rifle Association
North American Bear Society
Rocky Mountain Elk Foundation
Safari Club International
Wildlife Legislative Fund of America

To my family and friends who have hunted with me, believed in me, and all who have shared the love of the outdoors with me.

Help to keep our hunting heritage alive!

North American Black Bear

"*Patience, persistence, and hard work will get you any trophy animal there is.*"

Bill Butler—1969

—My lifetime hunting motto—

ABOUT THE COVERS

FRONT COVER:

Upper left-hand corner: Aoudad ram taken in Davis Mountains of west Texas.

Upper right-hand corner: Mountain goat taken in Rock Creek Drainage, Beartooth Mountains, Montana.

Lower left-hand corner: Mountain lion taken in Benbow Mine area of Beartooth Mountains, Montana.

Lower right-hand corner: Mule deer taken in Stillwater Canyon, Beartooth Mountains, Montana.

BACK COVER:

Upper left-hand corner: Boone & Crockett 86 point Antelope taken in Rosebud County, Montana.

Upper right-hand corner: SCI #7 Javelina taken in Chiricahua Mountains, Arizona.

Lower left-hand corner: Black bear taken in Saskatchewan, Canada.

Lower right-hand corner: Barren ground caribou taken near Lake Iliamna, Alaska.

These photos are duplicated later in the book with more complete information.

ALL PHOTOS IN BOOK BY AUTHOR.
(Except photos on pages 94, 98, 99, 100, 101, 102, 103 by James F. Butler)

AUTHOR'S NOTE: Hunters have only been required to wear fluorescent orange in Montana since 1972. Some states and provinces do not require that you wear any bright colors while hunting, that is why it is lacking in some photos.

ABOUT THE AUTHOR

Bill Butler, a former guide for 20 years, has himself taken over 60 trophies that qualify for Safari Club International Record Book, and several that make Boone & Crockett records; among them are a 42" Stone Sheep scoring 175 Boone & Crockett points, a 17" Antelope scoring 82-2/8, another Antelope scoring 86 B&C which is the fourth largest ever taken in Montana, and in 1992, a Wyoming antelope scoring 80-6/8 and a Montana antelope scoring 83-6/8 B&C both taken less than a month apart, a 7-1/2' Black Bear scoring 20-6/16 B&C, a huge Bison scoring 117 B&C, and a 392 B&C Barren Ground Caribou.

He is the first man to take all of Montana's big game animals, "The Big Ten". In the order he took them the collection includes, mule deer, pronghorn, black bear, white-tailed deer, elk, bighorn sheep, grizzly bear, moose, mountain goat and mountain lion. Bill has taken five bighorn sheep in Montana's unlimited area, and guided for several more. He has taken the Grand Slam of North American Deer. Bill also hunts predators, small game, waterfowl, upland birds, and wild turkeys. He fishes and writes in his spare time.

Bill Butler has appeared in the following magazines: Outdoor Life, Petersen's Hunting, Western Outdoors, Gun Digest, Gun Week, Fins and Feathers, Rocky Mountain Hunting and Fishing, Mike Eastman's Outdoorsmen, North American Hunting Club, and Boone & Crockett Quarterly, as well as numerous newspapers around the Rocky Mountain region.

He is an official measurer for the Boone & Crockett Club, Safari Club International, Foundation for North American Wild Sheep, Long Hunter's Society, and Rowland Ward Record Books.

Bill started the Montana Chapter of Safari Club International in 1980, was first President, and is still a member. He is a life member of the Foundation for North American Wild Sheep and the National Rifle Association. Bill is also a member of the Rocky Mountain Elk Foundation, the North American Hunting Club, North American Bear Society, and Montana Authors Coalition, Inc.

Bill has hunted extensively in North America, mostly self-guided. He has conducted many seminars on trophy hunting and is quoted in several other trophy hunting books.

TABLE OF CONTENTS

PREFACE

I have a lifetime of hunting experience, being born January 27, 1946, I am 47 years old as I write this. I shot my first big game animal when I was 12 years old. Before that I was going with my dad on his hunts from about age four. I have taken over 100 head of big game animals, mostly trophy class. I have hunted most of these animals on my own. When you hunt self-guided on your own, you learn how to hunt the animals you seek. It is not easy to start from scratch and learn how to hunt a particular species of animal on your own, but to me there is much satisfaction in taking your own game without a guide.

Because of the sheer volume of time spent seeking these animals in nature, you learn a lot about them and enjoy some great country along the way.

I am extremely lucky, I'll admit, but I have noticed that the harder I work both physically and mentally, the luckier I become. Hunting is my life, has always been, and hopefully always will be. When I am not hunting, I miss the wildness, the beauty, the freedom, the roaming.

This book is a partial history of my life as a hunter, and how I have been able to take 60 record class animals. I am talking about my own personal experiences, the details of many hunts, the techniques, the secrets, the trials and tribulations. If you read and study carefully, you can share my secrets for hunting super trophies. This is an overview of my hunting career, so that I can share with you how I learned to hunt from my very earliest memories onward.

A human hunter is an instinctual hunter from birth, as is a hunting dog, wolf, bear, coyote, fox, mountain lion, eagle, hawk, falcon, wolverine, mink, shark, or any other predator. Humans have been predators for as long as they have been on earth, some say about four million years. Man has been a predator for a lot longer than he has been able to not be one. Some men have a primal drive to hunt as does a wild predator.

I have had a keen interest in wild animals and wild places for as long as I can remember. I was shy as a boy. I loved to be alone, to wander the prairies, the fields, and river bottom woods near my Montana home. At first I carried only a stick on my expeditions to the wilds. To a very young boy, a several hour trip to a nearby woods was a major experience, a time for learning, exploring, and unconsciously getting in tune and step with the outdoors until you were one with nature.

There were cattail ringed ponds; with leopard frogs croaking, and painted turtles lazing away the day on a floating log, a muskrat swimming slowly by, ruddering with his tail, some bluewing teal and their young taking their living from the muddy water, the killdeer and other shorebirds running on the blue mud flats, and a redtail hawk shrieking occasionally and diving to carry away a field mouse for its young to eat, back at the nest. There were mink and raccoon tracks on the edge of the mud near the banks, that were lined behind the cattails, with red willows. Then there were the cottonwoods, small trees nearer the water, and on solid ground the large 100 footers over 100 years old. There in the brush, blending with nature, was the small boy, hiding, watching in awe, this beautiful spectacle on a warm breezeless summer afternoon.

Nature in all of its forms thrilled and exhilarated me then as it still does now. I enjoy all days, rain or shine, long or short, blistering hot or bitter cold. There are no bad days to me when I'm able to be close to nature in any form.

I am a naturalist that also hunts. Besides an intense interest in big game, I also study trees, flowers, and insects. I know the names of many. I keep a life list of North American birds and have personally identified 330+ different species to date.

I have introduced my wife, Diana, to bird watching as another way for us to spend more time together. Her life list is over 220+ in just a few years.

I enjoy fishing also. I have caught many species of fish. I like to eat fish, but have returned many to the water, unharmed. I trophy hunt while fishing also. I only keep what we can eat, or if I catch a really big one, I might have it mounted.

I was raised in a small town in south central Montana, only a few miles from where I now live.

Bill Butler - January 1993
Edgar, Montana

INTRODUCTION

Bill Butler is a great hunter and he has been blessed in many ways. He grew up in Montana -- that was a plus. The Montana he knew was blessed with 10 big game species that could be legally hunted -- he chased them all. And he grew up loving to hunt -- Lord, how the man loved to hunt.

In a way, it's just that simple. You might say that Bill becoming a great hunter was inevitable, just because of these parts of his existence. The truth of the matter, however, is that there were many Montanans who came of hunting age in the late 1950s who could have done the same thing. They could have honed their skills through the 1960s. They could have taken trophies in the 1970s, '80s and into the '90s. But few of Bill's contemporaries have matched his feats. Why? What's the difference between Bill and the others?

I suppose you'd have to go back to Bill's boyhood to get the first clue. Technically, he grew up in the tiny town of Silesia, Montana. But actually, he grew up in the fields, the woods and the mountains around Silesia. Every spare minute was spent in the outdoors he loved.

Though he was tall and strong and an enviable football prospect, the autumns of his high school years were spent hunting. He did go out for football for a time, and he rodeoed, too, but those activities would cease once hunting season began.

His desire to learn more about the outdoors and the creatures that lived in it consumed him. He learned the ways of the white-tailed deer in the river bottoms. He climbed above timberline to learn more about bighorn sheep and mountain goats. He walked the trails of black bears and grizzlies. He stalked the open plains of every fall of pronghorn antelope. And he climbed the snowy mountains of November when the big mule deer bucks and heavy-antlered bull elk were on the move toward their winter ranges.

Along the way, he endured the harsh blizzards of the high plateaus of sheep country, crept around buzzing rattlesnakes to move in on big antelope and pinched his pennies to expand his hunting horizons to other parts of the United States, Canada and countries beyond.

It's a trophy hunter's path that Bill followed. It's one that he has followed well enough so that his name is written into the record books of the Boone and Crockett Club and Safari Club International not once, but many times.

If there's a difference between Bill and many of the other trophy hunters, however, it's that for the most part, he has put his name there by himself. In all his years of hunting, he's only been on a handful of guided hunts. All but a few of his trophies have been on do-it-yourself hunts in Montana and elsewhere.

Bill has accomplished his feats based on his own hunting skills, his own knowledge of wildlife and without the fat wallets that many hunters require to put their names in the record books. To me, that makes him a rare individual indeed. He is truly a self-made hunter and a great one at that.

Now 47 years old, he's showing few signs of slowing down in his hunting. Just last fall, he took pronghorn antelope in both Montana and Wyoming that earned mention in Boone and Crockett. He passed up shots at mule deer bucks in Wyoming that most other hunters only dream about while searching for a really big one. And he managed to sneak in a few other hunts for bighorn sheep and whitetail deer, too.

How rare is the hunter who does these things? Suffice it to say that in more than 20 years as outdoor editor of the Billings Gazette, I've seen few others like him. He has a burning love of wildlife and a desire to hunt that can be matched by only a handful of hunters I've met in the past two decades. In the year's I've been in the writing business, I can also tell you that most hunting literature is written by great writers who hunt. Only rarely do you find work by great hunters who write. And Bill is undeniably a great hunter.

So read the stories that follow in this book very closely. You're tracking the history of a great hunter here. If you read the things Bill tells you and tap into the thinking between the lines, you can't help but become a better hunter yourself.

Mark Henckel
Park City, Montana

T.S. Bateman

Chapter 1

MY LUCKY DAY

In the cool of the evening, the antelope buck looked good. With the spotting scope turned up to sixty power, I could see that he had horns of at least 15-1/2 inches in length with long prongs and heavy bases. The sun was down now and the strong smells of the prairie; the sage, the grasses, and the cool dirt, drifted pleasantly upward to my nostrils.

The buck was a long ways away, at the bottom edge of where some rolling hills met the valley floor. He was definitely worth a closer look in the morning.

It was October 12, 1989, the fifth day of antelope season in Montana and my tag was still not filled.

I had been going from ranch to ranch looking for a Boone and Crockett size buck since the first day of the season on October 8. I had glassed thousands of antelope and hundreds of bucks, passing many bucks that I as a younger hunter would have shot for a wall mount and winter meat.

I had taken sixteen antelope bucks that qualified for Safari Club International's Record Book. One of these, a 17 incher, also made Boone and Crockett, with an official score of 82-2/8 points. Another massive old buck missed the Boone and Crockett awards book by three-eighths of an inch. One year I took a four-horned pronghorn antelope, an extreme rarity, a recessive genetic trait going back 25,000 years.

Montana is typically not known as a trophy antelope state, because the tough winters usually kill off the old bucks before they can reach their maximum potential. Montana has had less severe winters lately, allowing more bucks to reach advanced age and grow larger horn size.

I was hunting the vast area of eastern Montana north of the Yellowstone River and east of the Bull Mountains in Hunting District 700.

I was hunting alone, as I usually do. I hunt alone not because I dislike people, but because of the freedom needed to take an oversize trophy animal. I decide where I go, how long I stay in an area, how long I glass a particular buck, when I eat, when I stop hunting, etc.

I had gone to bed early that night in the nineteen foot travel trailer that I use as a camp. After many years of sleeping on the ground while hunting all of Montana's ten species of big game, I figure I deserve the luxury of a trailer for a camp for hunting animals such as antelope.

I arose early the next morning and after a brief breakfast, I drove in the dark to where I had been the night before as I glassed the large buck.

The eastern horizon was just starting to gray.

I sat quietly in the Ford pickup considering the prospects for the day. I don't play the radio because in the extreme stillness of early morning, noise carries a long distance to wary animals' ears.

The sky grew paler and I could see individual clumps of bunch grass. The saffron color was next and it soon spread across the sky enough that I would now be able to start glassing.

I stepped out of the pickup into the cool, sharp air. "Thank you God for down jackets", I thought.

Glassing first with my 10x25 Zeiss binoculars, I swept everything in view of my position, making mental notes of the antelope herds. Next I set up the spotting scope and studied the individual herds for bucks. These I studied until I was satisfied they were not what I wanted in a trophy buck. I don't give a second look to anything under fourteen inches long. Above that I consider horn length, prong length, and overall mass.

A small stream near me sparkled among the sage.

I quickly located the large buck from the night before. He was out at about six hundred yards. There were no other large bucks showing.

Around dawn, antelope don't seem to pay much attention to a vehicle at long range. Following a ranch road, I drove out of the buck's sight up a long valley. I then drove to within a half a mile of the feeding buck while behind a ridge line. Here I parked the pickup, just off the side of the small road, and sneaked over to the edge for a look. The clear, Indian summer day was unfolding beautifully.

From this new vantage point, I scanned everything I could see again, first with the binoculars, then with the Bausch and Lomb 15x60 spotting scope. My large buck of the night before was feeding at about 600 yards. No closer than before, but now I was above him and had a ridge to use as concealment while I stalked him. He was actually off the end of the long finger ridge in front of me.

There was a large herd of antelope headed for a morning drink at a reservoir on the right side of the ridge. The wind was from that direction also. "This is good", I thought, "they can't see or smell me". I planned to stay on the left side of the ridge to stalk the buck. Then near the end of the ridge, but on the left side where I planned to stalk, I saw five antelope. There were four does and a buck. I studied the buck in the spotting scope. He looked extremely heavy horned, but short in horn length. He was feeding by himself about a hundred yards from the does. I had seen an extremely heavy horned antelope in the area for the previous two hunting seasons. That buck was short horned, probably thirteen inches plus, with short prongs. His horns swept back in a distinctive way. This new buck had fairly good prongs, maybe the same buck, just older, more developed. I had to get closer to check him out

18

Montana's number 4 Antelope.

and the other big buck I had been previously glassing that morning. The only way to get closer would be to crawl on my stomach down the narrow flat area that ran the length of the top of the 500 yard long ridge. If I didn't crawl, the antelope on either side would see me.

The sage covered valley ahead of me was taking on a grey-green look in the rising sun's light.

I crawled on my belly using my elbows and knees to move me along. I had my binoculars inside my shirt, my rifle slung on my back and the spotting scope and small tripod in one hand. I carefully negotiated my way amongst the cactus, picking up one of the white spines now and then anyway. I would stop and pluck it out unless it was broken off and would have to be tended to later. I kept a sharp eye out for rattlesnakes also. Three different times previously while hunting, rattlesnakes had struck at me, missing me twice, and hitting me on a boot top the third time, but not penetrating the leather or doing any damage to me. I watch closely for these vicious reptiles of the prairie.

After crawling for quite a distance, I crawled to the side of the ridge top to look at the antelope to see what they were doing. The four does were just feeding over a small rise and joined the larger herd at the end of the ridge that contained the first longer horned buck. The buck with the shorter, heavier, horns was slowly feeding that way also. The buck looked extremely heavy horned at this closer range. I watched the buck for about ten minutes, until he fed over out of sight with the main herd. Now the bucks would be together and after crawling the remaining distance, I peeked around a sage brush to compare the two. Both bucks were feeding with the herd about 200 yards from me. The longer horned buck looked to be about 15-1/2 inches long, with a five inch prong and moderately heavy bases. He would score about 78 or 79 points. The other buck looked extremely heavy but short horned in proportion to his face length and body size.

I am a Boone and Crockett scorer and have scored a large number of antelope heads. I had a dilemma now though. The heavy buck looked like he might be only a little over 13 inches long. The horns appeared to have a gray tint to them. Real heavy horns usually look black. He had a good prong and was heavy above the prong also. I glassed both bucks again and again. I just kept looking at the heavy buck and I didn't know how big he was. I knew that to be a good judge of an antelope like this one was critical if I wanted to make the book again. If I misjudged and shot him he might be smaller than I thought. If he turned out to be bigger, then that would be okay though. I was trying to make up my mind whether to shoot the buck or pass him up when the other long horned buck walked by the heavy horned buck. The heavy horned buck was about a third larger in body and head size than the long horned buck. I knew instantly that the heavy horned buck was a giant. His horns were extra large, only looking smaller because of his large head and body size. I knew that I must shoot him. While I moved from my spotting scope to my rifle, the heavy horned buck laid down quartering toward me. None of the antelope had seen me and the wind was in my favor, so I watched the large buck for a few minutes. The buck suddenly got up and started to walk from left to right. The wind hadn't changed and the antelope couldn't see me, maybe a sixth sense warned him.

I held the 3x9 Leupold's cross hairs behind the buck's shoulders and fired. The 180 grain, 30.06 bullet found its mark, the buck immediately going down. I got up and walked to the buck as the other antelope sped away. The buck was built like a bulldog. He was big and heavily muscled, the largest bodied antelope I had ever taken. He later weighed 101 pounds, compared to a typical antelope that weighs 70 pounds field dressed. The horns had bases of 8-3/8 inches with the horns being 14-7/8 and 14-3/8 inches long. They carried extremely heavy with the prongs being 6 inches long and 5-2/8 inches long.

After 60 days drying, another Boone and Crockett scorer totaled the buck at 86 Boone and Crockett points. This would make him number four from Montana for all time. If he had not broken 3/4 of an inch off the one prong so that it matched the unbroken one, he would have scored an amazing 87-1/2 points.

On the way home after shooting the antelope I heard on the radio that it was an unlucky day. I just laughed. I shot the big antelope on Friday the 13th. Unlucky for the antelope yes, but it was my lucky day.

"I know that I have an instinctive sixth sense while hunting. Others say I'm just lucky, but I know better. After following my hunches for this long and being successful, I think I will continue to trust my sixth sense."

Bill Butler
February 1993

I shot this 16-1/2 inch antelope on October 28, 1990 in Rosebud County, Montana. The horns score 79 points in SCI Record Book. I did my preseason scouting and couldn't find a decent buck. The season opened and I hunted hard for four days. I located a good buck that had a couple of inches broken off of one horn tip. I decided to pass on shooting the buck, but pointed it out to another hunter. He made a good stalk and shot the buck. It would have scored 81 points if it didn't have the broken horn. My King of the Mountain camouflage wool clothing is warm and quiet in the outdoors. The Blowdown pattern of grays and browns blends well in mountains, woodlands, river bottoms and prairies.

Continued from previous page. This is the only animal in this book of which two different photos appear. This photo of the short nosed antelope buck shows how long a 16-1/2 inch horn can appear if it doesn't have much hook at the tip. This buck's horns have good length and long prongs but lack extreme mass, keeping it out of Boone & Crockett. After my poor start that season, I hunted several more times without success. I shot a doe antelope on a doe tag so I would have antelope meat for the winter. Antelope start loosing their horns near the first of November, and I was getting worried. This buck was traveling, and walked right to me on an expansive "pancake flat" prairie. PERSISTENCE.

This was my first trip to Alaska. My brother Doug and I hunted together for moose. I spotted this bull one day and thought I would stockpile him for later if I didn't find a bigger one. Instead, I told Doug to go get him and he did. I didn't find my bigger one and should have shot this one, plenty big for a first one. The bull was 58 inches wide and had wide palms with 25 points. The bull fell seven miles from the lake where we were camped and there was a lot of meat packing before we got him out. Doug has since taken several other big moose, black bear, and a Boone & Crockett Record Book caribou in Alaska.

My research on trophy Sitka Blacktail Deer led me to Terror Bay, Alaska. I rode the ferry boat from Homer to Kodiak Island. On the way I saw humpbacked whales, sea otters, tufted puffins, sea lions and seals. A float plane dropped me at a small lake high on the mountain. A biologist had told me that there were over 100 Alaska Brown Bears eating salmon on a two mile stretch of river below where I would camp, but I didn't see any up high. I saw 15 mature bucks a day above timberline, on the rolling, volcanic mountain. I shot my 5x5 at 50 yards on August 21st, boned the meat and packed it to my camp. The buck was number 15 in Safari Club Record Book and missed Boone & Crockett by 3/8 of an inch.

T.S.Bateman

After the Blacktail Deer hunt, my bush pilot brother, Doug, dropped me near Lake Iliamna to hunt Barren Ground Caribou. One day I hunted out as far as I thought I could go and still get back to my camp by dark, but then I saw four tremendous bull caribou through my spotting scope over a mile away. Knowing I would have to spend the night away from camp, I started to stalk the bachelor group. I used the rolling terrain for cover and stalked upwind to within 100 yards and shot the biggest bull. I spent the night with no supper, wrapped in my space blanket under a thick spruce tree. The bull had 43 points and makes Boone & Crockett Awards and Safari Club Record Books. It was August 30.

The Dominant Black Wolf.

"To hunt true trophy animals on your own, you must have natural talent, extreme discipline, intelligence, perseverance, ambition, a strong measure of common sense, and confidence in knowing that there are massive and unique trophy animals actually out there to be taken. You must possess these qualities and believe in your heart that you can actually attain your trophy, to be consistently successful."

Bill Butler-Dec. 1992

Chapter 2

WOLF KILL

The raw violence overpowered me, the frantic cries screamed at my ears as she struggled for her life. Her mother having outran her; without ever looking back, left her to be the killers' victim. My skin was drawn tight and my hands throbbed from the supercharge of adrenalin that primes one for split second fight or flight. There was nothing I could do for her as I watched helplessly from a half a mile away.

Just previous to this drama I had been hunting in northern British Columbia for several days and had shot a 42" stone ram that green scored 177 points, qualifying him for the all-time Boone & Crockett Record Book. He was a beautiful, silver faced, black ram with a large body that I would later have mounted life size.

We had now been hunting mountain caribou for the last couple of days. I had seen an extra large bull earlier in the hunt but had passed it up for fear of scaring a ram with the shot. I had also passed several big bulls with broken horns.

It was past mid-October now and the morning dawned gray and cold. After a very hearty breakfast of bacon, hot cakes, coffee, eggs, and fried potatoes, we saddled the horses and rode up canyon.

We tied the horses at the entrance to a large side canyon and proceeded on foot from there. The mouth of the side canyon had rocky escarpments on each side for about a half a mile, and then opened out into a large basin. After the cliffs ended, the main basin's terrain was made up of fine shale and dark soil, covered here and there with short brush, a few short wind stunted pine trees, and brown grass. There was a cover of about four inches of fresh snow from the night before.

As myself, the guide, and the wrangler climbed up the side canyon, three mountain goats got up, above us and to our right. The two nannies and a kid were in the rocks and headed out, up the basin.

We climbed high enough up onto the smooth right side of the basin to have a commanding view of the whole basin. We glassed for mountain caribou but didn't see any.

I saw the three mountain goats go out of sight over a pass at the head of the basin three-quarters of a mile away. We were sitting in some short snow covered brush just glassing the surrounding hills.

We had concluded that there were no caribou in the basin.

I happened to glass back to the pass where the goats had disappeared only a few minutes earlier. There, coming as fast as they could run, were the three goats. I pointed them out to the other two woodsmen. The mountain goats were running along the far side of the basin, making for the rocky cliffs across from our position. Then I noticed more movement at the pass at the head of the basin. I watched as four timber wolves appeared, running headlong after the fleeing goats. The goats had run right into the wolves just over the pass and the goats now were running for their lives. The closest rocks and safety for the goats were over a half a mile away.

The lead wolf, a lean and racy slate gray, was about a hundred yards ahead of the next two wolves. These two were normal gray colored wolves with one of them having distinctive white markings on its face. Bringing up the rear, about 200 yards back of the two grays, was a big, extremely black wolf. It lumbered along slowly, probably a big male.

We watched in awe as the greyhound looking, slate wolf closed on the terrified goats. The goats were fast, but the yellow-eyed slate was faster. Just before the goats reached the sanctuary of the cliffs, the slate turned the kid back and ran it right into one of the gray wolves' waiting jaws. From a half a mile away, we could hear the young kid goat's anguished cries.

The wolves had increased to three now. The slate racer held to the front of the pitiful victim while the two grays disemboweled it. I could see patches of white hide being thrown 15 feet in the air as the cries continued. I was rivetted to my glasses as the fury went on for about 10 seconds and then all was quiet. The three ate rapidly, ripping at the rear quarters of the warm goat carcass.

Momentarily, the big black male arrived and his dominance was clearly shown as the other three wolves drew back and waited while he ate.

After watching the chase, my own predator instinct was aroused and I felt as excited as the wolves. I had bought wolf tags earlier and now told the guide, an experienced northern hunter, that I wanted to try to stalk the wolves for a shot. The guide and wrangler both laughed at me and expounded on the wolf's wildness, wariness, alertness and a human's inability to approach one undetected.

While moving slowly so as not to be noticed, I removed my down jacket, wool shirt and white longjohn top. Then I recovered myself with first my wool shirt, then my down jacket and then over everything, my white longjohn top. Improvised snow camouflage in short order!

I had on Pendleton wool pants that were about the same color as the brush, a mauvish gray/brown. My down cap was also about the color of the brush. The brush that we were sitting in was about knee high.

I cradled my rifle in my arms and slowly slipped and slithered down through the brush for a couple hundred yards to the bottom of the basin.

Here I eased into a dry water course that was about three feet deep and blown in with snow. I very laboriously crawled along in the soft snow in the direction of the wolves. I had tape on the end of my barrel to keep out the snow and also had my scope covers on.

When I figured my position was even with the wolves' location on the hillside above me, I stopped and peeked over the lip of the trough, looking through a bush to conceal me.

The wolves were on a slight bench about 250 yards above me. Only their backs were visible from my position. The black was still feeding alone at the carcass.

There was a small, dense wind stunted pine about 75 yards from me and almost in line with the wolves. I lined myself up behind the diminutive pine and crawling when the wolves heads were down, was soon at the tree. I was now 175 yards from the wolves. I could only see the back of the black one.

I rested my rifle over a low branch, positioning it close to the tree trunk. I pushed the safety off and laid waiting in the snow, as cocked and ready as the rifle. I didn't have to wait long. The black wolf finished eating and took a few steps out to the edge of the bench and stood broadside facing to my left. I held on his lungs but just as I pulled the trigger, the wolf stepped forward.

I didn't hear the bullet hit him and as I swiftly regained my sight picture after the recoil, I saw the large black disappear to my right into a thin finger of timber.

At this same instant, the white faced gray wolf ran into my sight picture and stopped. I centered the crosshairs on it but didn't shoot. Thinking that I might have missed the black wolf with my first shot, I didn't want to miss a split second chance for a second shot because the black was the one I really wanted. I looked for the black but couldn't see it.

Before I had time to regret not shooting at the gray, I saw the agile slate colored wolf flying down the hill toward me in a blind escape run. The slate's appearance was so fast, and surprising that I couldn't get off a shot as it passed within 15 feet of me. I quickly turned and started shooting at the swift slate as it streaked down the hill and up the other side.

The northern guides speak of the good luck that wolves have when being shot at. I shot four times at the racer and hit so close that the wolf changed directions with each shot, but I didn't cut a hair on it. This wolf was soon out of range and I turned back to see if I could spot any of the other wolves.

The two grays were long gone, but there slowly loping straight away from me was the dominant black. Because of his extremely slow gait, I thought he was probably hit. He was out at about 400 yards now. I allowed for bullet drop and tried to estimate the correct lead. At the shot the wolf swapped ends and came running back toward me. The bullet had kicked up snow in front of him, causing his reversal of direction. I held my fire and let him come toward me.

When he was about 250 yards from me, the black wolf turned abruptly to my left without breaking stride and headed across, angling up the slope. I swung my rifle on him again and fired. I saw the wolf's hind leg dip at the shot, but he kept running as strongly as he had been running before the shot. I knew I had hit him and now also knew my correct hold for lead.

The ebony giant was just heading over the last crest at about 250 yards and I knew it was now or never. At the shot the wolf went out of sight over the rise. I jumped to my feet and stood peering in the direction he had disappeared. Then I saw his tail flip in the air and he kicked and came rolling back down the hill toward me.

About this time I heard whooping and hollering from my cheering section a half a mile away.

I had retrieved the wolf and the kid goat by the time the guide and wrangler arrived. My first shot had hit the wolf just back of the diaphragm and would have eventually killed him. The second shot only cut the skin on the outside of his hock, but the resulting, momentary falter in his gate told me my lead was close to being right. My last shot went through his shoulders, putting him down.

After hearty congratulations by the other two and statements that they didn't believe it and they didn't think it could be done, we tagged the wolf, photographed it, and skinned it. I took the skull also.

I couldn't find a good caribou bull, but was plenty happy with a 42" stone ram and a black wolf anyway.

Wolves are not an endangered species in Canada or Alaska.

Mountain lion taken by Diana Butler and her Walker hound, Ridge, on January 18, 1994, near the Beartooth Mountains of Montana. The mature tom lion was the first for both Diana and Ridge. Bill and another friend and his dog, Jake, helped on the all-day hunt. Mountain lion meat is excellent table fare with a pleasant taste and texture.

Chapter 3

"WIND WHISPER"

"Wind Whisper" is the best, most accurate, wind directional indicator ever made. If you don't keep track of the wind while you are hunting, you probably only take game in situations where the wind is accidentally in your face, through no cause of your own. Keeping track of wind direction is one of the most important things a hunter must do. With the "Wind Whisper", you can secretly tell wind direction by moving only your eyes.

The "Wind Whisper", made of synthetic unwaxed dental floss, is extremely sensitive, and can detect even the slightest breeze. The "Wind Whisper" is resistant to rain and snow, and is no more visible to animals than a cobweb hanging from a limb. The "Wind Whisper" is also quiet, absolutely soundless. The "Wind Whisper" is easy to install. You place it on a rifle barrel, bow limb, camera, or tripod and secure with tape.

Many people try to detect wind direction by sifting dust or crumbling leaves through their fingers, or use a squeeze bottle of talc. This is messy, inaccurate, and most importantly, requires movement. Also, with a bottle of talc, you have something else to carry, when you don't have enough room in your pockets for the important things anyway.

If you are on a stand or are still hunting or stalking, you have to be extremely careful to not make unnecessary movements. With "Wind Whisper" you only have to move your eyes to tell exactly which way the wind is blowing.

Before discovering the material for my "Wind Whisper", I tried many unsuitable materials and methods for detection of wind direction. I have tried yarn which attracts moisture and is heavy and insensitive to gentle breezes. I tried fishing line and it is too stiff and doesn't have enough surface area to catch wind well. Bow string silencers are made of rubber or yarn and are too heavy to catch gentle breezes. Common strings are too heavy also. Thread is too light and wraps around your barrel. Puff bottles require too much movement. Wetting a finger, then holding it in the wind to tell direction can be inaccurately interpreted up to 30 degrees in error either way from the correct wind direction. This error is critical if you are making a cross wind stalk. You have only 45 degrees to work with totally to begin with, but if you make a 30 degrees error, then you have only 15 degrees remaining margin for error. A fickle wind can easily change 15 degrees and spook your quarry. A stalker, still hunter, or stand hunter of any animal that depends on its nose to detect danger can increase their chances of success anytime they go afield by using a "Wind Whisper".

Here's how to make your own "Wind Whisper":

1.   Start with an 8 inch piece of unwaxed dental floss.

2.   Now tie a clinch knot in one end, and before pulling the clinch knot tight, put the loose end or opposite end back through the clinch knot. This will leave you with a loop at one end of the piece of floss.

3.   Next, lay the floss on a hard surface, such as a dining table or countertop. Draw a very dull table knife (without serrations) from the looped end towards the loose end. Repeat about three times and watch as the strands unravel and become parallel instead of twisted as they were to start with. Don't overdue this step because you need some twists to keep the floss in more or less one linear piece. Over time this allows the floss to expand, causing it to develop a larger area to be exposed to the wind.

4.   Now you slip the loop over your gun barrel and pull the loop tight. You can put a spot of super glue on the knot to keep it from loosening. If you have a front sight on your rifle barrel, you won't have to worry about the "Wind Whisper" slipping off. If you don't have a front sight, just secure the "Wind Whisper" near the end of the barrel with a piece of tape.

Let this helpful little device whisper to you about the wind.

Mountain Lion

38

The Montana Grizzly Bear was a real tough animal for me to collect. Before they quit the hunting season on them, grizzlies were harder to get a look at than a big whitetail buck. They were skittish and shy. Grizzlies are very intelligent and if they don't want you to see them, then you usually won't. I hunted every day for five weeks one year, and never saw a live grizzly, only tracks. I played cat and mouse with a big boar grizzly with a 12 inch long track, in some thick timber but never saw him, let alone got a shot. PATIENCE, PERSISTENCE, HARD WORK. I didn't give up but kept hunting hard and covering the country. I got lucky the next year and found this bear on the first day of the backcountry season, September 15th. I knew from the tracks that there were grizzlies in the area. I was hiding behind a log watching a trail and an open hillside below me late one evening. This grizzly bear came down the trail below, crossing the hillside only 25 yards below my position. I shot it through the lungs with a 220 grain bullet from my 30-06. The grizzly rolled a few yards down the hill and immediately after stopping, located me and came back up the hill with its jaws snapping loudly and growling ferociously. I was ready to shoot again but the angry bear collapsed and died with its enraged eyes still locked on me.

The Grizzly Bear that I shot was a part of a group of mature bears. Within minutes after I shot my bear, I saw three more mature grizzlies come out at the upper end of the meadow, acting agitated and snapping their teeth. After field dressing I dragged my bear out of there as fast as I could go, arriving at my vehicle well after dark. One of the grizzly bears was real big, bigger than my bear. I went out to Cooke City that night and called my brother Doug and told him to get up here right away because I had killed a grizzly bear and had seen three more. The next day we went back to the place where I had field dressed my grizzly and the other grizzlies had eaten their friend's remains. We could see where the bears had followed me the night before, stepping on top of my tracks. We hunted the country hard for several days and finally on the fifth day, had the three grizzlies walk out in front of us across an alpine meadow. At a 100 yards, Doug dropped the biggest grizzly, but it got up and ran. Doug hit it again as it ran and it went down for a second time. He put another 175 grain 7 mag bullet into the bear for good measure as it lay there. The grizzly jumped to its feet and ran into the timber. We tracked it into the timber where Doug shot it a fourth time killing it.

I shot this Montana Whitetail Buck on November 3, in the same meadow where I shot my first whitetail buck 5 years before. This buck was a 5x6 that field dressed 180 lbs. and qualifies for SCI Record Book. As a method of hunting, I have tried tracking down a whitetail buck, but where I hunt them here, there are cattle, sheep, big rivers, etc. that cause you a lot of trouble. I have tracked down mule deer bucks in the snow and shot them, usually catching them within two miles. I shot this buck from a large cottonwood tree. I don't use man-made tree stands if I don't have to, but prefer to just climb up a tree about 30 feet and stand on a large limb. This can sometimes be dangerous though. My reason for not using a man-made tree stand is to keep my hunting area secret from other hunters. If I have put a lot of work into finding a big buck, I don't want some other fellow to move in and start hunting him also. I stalk my tree stand as quietly as possible so I don't frighten any deer that may be laying within earshot. I try to arrive at the tree about two hours before dark, so that the animals forget about me by the time they get up to feed. If you show up late, the bucks will not get out of their beds until after full darkness. Don't use any aftershave, cologne, or scented lotions before going hunting. The scent from these will stay with you several days, allowing deer to smell you.

4x2 Whitetail Buck that I shot from a cottonwood tree.

"Hunting is the most real thing I have ever done. The planning, the anticipation, the relentless seeking, the game animals, the chase, the kill, the providing. This is the essence of life to one born a predator."

Bill Butler-December 31, 1992

Chapter 4

RIGHT-HANDED SHOT
AT A WRONG THINKING BUCK

I did not know it at the time, but the five point whitetail buck lay bedded in thick brush near my tree stand as I sneaked through the bright November afternoon. I walked slowly stopping often, looking deeply into the thick tangles of underbrush in the cottonwood forest for a leg, an ear, an antler, or the reddish brown color that would give a deer's presence away. I pushed briars out of my way so that they would not scrape on my pant legs. I placed my feet carefully so not to step on any dry branches. I reached the tree about three hours before dark and climbed as quietly as possible to a fork about thirty feet above ground.

The time passed slowly, but beautifully. The mountains in the distance were snowy and brilliantly blue when I arrived. As twilight neared, they became darker, larger and more ominous looking. In the fading light of the Montana sky, two rooster pheasants crowed from separate locations. Then came together in the meadow for a short sparring match. The winner strutted with tail feathers erected at a 45 degree angle and his head bobbed as he looked for another challenger, while his defeated foe moved to another area that he could dominate.

A large flock of Canada geese flew up the river towards a feeding ground, honking loudly. Three Mallard ducks, two hens and a drake, wheeled in to light on a deep pool in the small, winding stream that passed beneath the tree stand. A whitetail doe and two fawns moved out into the edge of the small enclosed meadow. One fawn carried nubbin horns beneath swirls of hair atop his head. A squirrel scrambled head first down a tree and started digging up his hidden treasures.

As darkness gathered, a skunk came steadily along one of the three trails that crossed beneath the weathered old tree and continued on until out of sight. A mink swam by and frightened the ducks from the pool.

The shooting light was all but gone when I heard the buck get up from his bed and move out onto the trail. He was coming from behind me slowly, stopping to smell of brush that I had touched. He had forgotten about my earlier presence by now and was not frightened but curious. I turned slowly in the tree to get the animal in my variable scope which was now turned down to 3 power. The buck had five well matched points on each side, but the beams were not very heavy or long, nor were the points long. He stopped to smell of the base of the tree and I removed my cap, held it as squarely above him as possible and then dropped it. It narrowly missed his rump. He jumped twenty feet, stood for a short time looking back and then grazed out into the meadow to join the other deer. I did not shoot him. He was not the big buck that I had glassed earlier in the summer and had now hunted for three weeks.

On the twenty-fifth day of sitting in the tree, a long bodied old whitetail buck with a large four point antler on one side and two non-typical horns growing straight in the air on the other side, trotted into the meadow. Three mule deer does had crossed the meadow just ahead of him. He was hot on their track. Alberta biologists have proven that whitetail and mule deer will cross.

I am a right-handed person, but my lead eye is my left one so I naturally grew up shooting left-handed. I shoot a right-handed bolt action rifle, left-handed. Because of the present position of the buck in relation to the direction grown by the heavy branch I was standing on, I would not be allowed to shoot left-handed. I laid down horizontally on the stout branch, then squirmed around to brace myself from falling off and also to get into a right-handed shooting position. Before the boom of the 30-06 settled away, I knew that the long sought trophy was mine.

Killing an animal is a small part of hunting to me. I personally would rather not shoot than kill a small, immature animal. When you can pass up a good specimen of your quarry that is still not the size you are searching for, after weeks of hunting through bad weather and good, after the long months through the off season spent trying to locate a real trophy animal, then you are well along in the sport of trophy hunting. The refusal to settle for less is the biggest step toward bringing home a trophy that will remain a great satisfaction.

HUNTING TIPS:

Wear polypropolene - wool headband to keep ears warm, with possibly a cap under it. You will be able to hear better through the headband than through ear flaps. I hear just fine with my King of the Mountain bomber hat though.

If you have lost a wounded animal before or during a snowstorm, you can backtrack a coyote or fox in the snow later and they will sometimes lead you to your downed trophy.

This is my first Whitetail Buck, a 6 x 6 that makes SCI Record Book. I shot it on October 28, 1964 after many years of trying to bag one of these elusive animals. In an area that I had roamed since childhood, I found an excess of buck rubs on trees near a small, secluded meadow. I sat in a tree for six evenings without seeing anything. Then one afternoon as I was approaching the meadow, I could see through the brush ahead of me, the head, horns, and neck of a whitetail buck at 130 yards. I got buck fever so bad, I had to sit down for a couple of minutes and calm myself before I could shoot the buck which field dressed 180 lbs. Doug heard the shot and came running to help me drag it.

Elusive Whitetail Buck

Chapter 5

FIELD JUDGING
TROPHY WHITETAIL BUCKS

VARIABLES AFFECTING FIELD JUDGING

1.   Distance to Trophy - Bucks look bigger real close. If a buck looks big at a great distance, in glasses or spotting scope, then it is big.

2.   Available Light - In dim light bucks look smaller. In bright light, against snow or on a skyline, bucks look bigger.

3.   Position of Animal - Bucks appear much larger when viewed from behind, but smaller when looking at them from above as from a tree stand.

4.   Body Size - Mature looking bucks are fuller bodied, with sagging belly and back. Older bucks look old and masculine with muscles showing. A young buck by contrast is sleek, flat backed and straight bellied with a streamlined look.

5.   Length of Time to Judge - If you know these judging tips by heart, then you may be able to make a quick judgment, but taking more time is always better.

6.   Visibility - Snow, rain, fog or brush can negatively affect accurate judging.

7.   Experience - Actual field experience of looking at many deer before and after a kill and scoring horns and mounted deer heads will help make a hunter more adept at judging big bucks also.

RACK CHARACTERISTICS TO CONSIDER
DURING FIELD JUDGING

1.   Antler Spread - This can be judged by ear spread which runs from 16 to 19 inches when alert. You should measure dead deer for experience on this. Many Boone & Crockett bucks are not wide, with inside antler spread of only 18 inches or less.

2.   Length of Points - Long points are very important to total score. There are almost always brow points on mature whitetail bucks.

3.   Number of Points - Three upright points on outer view of main beam. This would make a buck a 5 x 5 point. Boone and Crockett has very few 4 x 4 bucks listed. A Boone and Crockett class typical has a fourth point of at least 6 inches in length and the previous ones will be longer.

Non-typicals are hard to judge accurately until they are shot and on the ground. A general rule is if you like the buck, shoot it.

4.   General Mass or Heaviness of Beams - Mass is the first thing you will notice about a buck's appearance. Mass contributes about 18% of the total score. There is not that much difference in the scores of a heavy buck and a light one.

5.   Hair Length - With short hair as in bow season or in Texas or Mexico a buck's horns look bigger. In late season in the north country like Montana, Alberta, etc., a buck that has a long winter coat has horns that appear smaller because of the hair length.

6.   Length of Main Beam - The average length of the main beam in the record book is 27-1/2 inches. From a side view, the main beams should extend past the nose or if a buck is exceptionally wide, the beam tips should hook in close to the center line of the head.

7.   A Generally Gnarled Formation - This condition denotes age. Canadian bucks are generally more massive and gnarly than United States bucks.

A big buck will be immediately recognizable to an experienced hunter of trophy bucks. I call these "one look bucks" because after only one glance, I know I want to collect this fine animal. These are the kind of trophy bucks I enjoy hunting most, they make my pulse quicken.

HUNTING TIPS:

A large trophy animal sinks further into the ground than a normal animal. In Saskatchewan once, I saw the day-old track of a huge black bear which had a six inch wide front pad and he sank two inches deep into the pine needles and soil. I weighed 250 lbs. at the time and I didn't leave a visible track.

If you are in a tree stand, and there are deer nearby, wait until the deer wander far enough away from your tree so that you don't alert them as you descend. This prevents you from educating the deer to the fact that hunters use tree stands.

If you hunt during rain or snow storms, the falling moisture takes your scent to the ground, allowing you to hunt downwind without alerting the animal to your presence.

I took this big 6x6 Whitetail Buck on November 24 on the Bighorn River in Montana. I had been after him for several days. He would go up into the ponderosa pine covered hills during the day and come down to his scrapes, the alfalfa fields, and does after dark. I found about 20 scrapes but couldn't get a look at the buck. He was leaving out before dawn each day. Then one frosty morning, because of heavy rutting activity, he stayed too long. I am still impressed by the memory of the frost covered alfalfa, and the frost on the buck's back and horns in the bright morning sunlight. I crawled several hundred yards in an irrigation ditch and shot the buck at 150 yards from a prone position.

I collected this 5x6 Whitetail Buck in Saskatchewan, Canada on December 3rd of the same year that I got the Bighorn River buck. The buck field dressed 220 lbs. and had forked brow points on each side. He was an old buck, past his prime. If his horns would have matched, he would have scored near 155 B&C points. It was about 20 degrees below zero and the hunting was crisp. The buck was after a doe in the second rut and was reluctant to leave her. I angled a bullet through him as he ran quartering away and to my right at 120 yards. I had to pick an opening between the birch trees and shoot quick. Being able to shoot quick and accurately offhand is very important in trophy hunting.

Happy looking fellow, must be sitting on a cactus! It's all right if you smile if you are happy with your trophy. When I was younger, I tried to emulate some of the old time hunters who never smiled. I always smile now, because I'm a Christian and have a lot to smile about. I shot this non-typical 7x4 whitetail in early November in Montana. The buck had 11 points on the one side, but broke all but four of them off. I was in a small cottonwood tree, up about 20 feet. There was a high wind blowing and the tree was waving around quite a bit. I was on a large island in the Clarks Fork River. This buck came out just before dark, 250 yards away across an abandoned field. He was trotting from left to right on a game trail that followed the river. I got the most solid hold I could get on the rifle, resting it over a branch, then waited for the wind to lull and fired. The buck dropped instantly. I'm a fairly good shot but sometimes luck helps a little too. Smart whitetail bucks will program you real quick and avoid your stand if you use the stand very often. Have at least a half a dozen different stands no closer than half a mile apart. Rotate and let each stand rest several days between use. To camouflage your scent, you can keep your hunting clothes in a plastic bag with pine boughs or sage leaves or whatever is common to your area and put them on when you arrive to hunt.

Mule Deer Buck

Hunting Tips

In extremely vast, thick cover, shoot any game animal through the shoulders so they drop immediately instead of running where you might not be able to find them after they die.

Always try to shoot dangerous game, such as grizzly bear, from above. Try to break down dangerous game animals with a shot through the shoulders so they won't be able to attack you as easily.

Chapter 6

MY FIRST GOOD MULE DEER

We were in the Pryor Mountains of Montana to hunt mule deer in the fall of 1964. It was early November and my brother, Doug, and I were camped at the fork of the roads where one road leads to the Dryhead Overlook and the other winds down Crooked Creek toward Lovell, Wyoming. A fresh snow had fallen each of the last two days and the sky at night was so cold, crisp and clear that it seemed as though you could reach up and touch the stars.

I would drive out each morning with the wet snow crunching solidly underneath the tires as I went. I parked my vehicle at the upper end of a deep canyon. With a couple of candy bars for lunch, I would walk along the rims very slowly, placing my feet carefully so as not to dislodge any rocks that might spook deer bedded below me in the timber. I could see into the timber on the far side of the canyon and studied it constantly as I stalked along, hoping to see a big buck.

I spotted some does and a couple of two-point bucks bedded down watching me, but nothing big. I could see into the timber below me on the same side of the canyon once in a while, but not very well. Rocky points jutted out occasionally from the rim and when I would come to one of these, I would have a good view of both sides of the canyon from the tips of them. I would walk out on the points as far as I could to glass.

I was about halfway between two of these rock outcroppings when I heard the brush breaking below me and slightly up canyon where I had just passed.

I saw a large mule deer doe come out of the timber in the bottom of the canyon and climb the far side a short distance to where she hit a game trail and turned down canyon to follow it. Seven more does and fawns followed her out of the timber and down the trail through the scattered timber. An average five-point buck trailed them. I was trying to size him up in my scope when I noticed the big buck leave the timber and scramble up to the trail. The deer would come through an opening about 20 yards wide directly across from me.

I sat down in the soft snow so I could rest my elbows over my knees for a steadier hold on the rifle. The deer came slowly but without stopping. They were not badly spooked. I could glance the big buck as he came across small openings as he followed the does. The does crossed the large opening across from me in single file with the mediocre buck right after them. They were gone about a minute when the big buck walked out to the middle of the opening, stopped and looked back up

6 x 6 Muley buck from the rimrocks.

canyon, wondering what had spooked the others. One look was all I needed. I placed the crosshairs behind his shoulder and let fire. He lunged and bucked like a wild horse as the rifle roared. Just as he went into the timber I could see him go down.

It took me about an hour to get to him because I had to walk down canyon until I could find a break in the rim where I could climb down. He had six long points on each side with heavy, dark colored beams that spread fairly wide. He gross scored about 180 non-typical Boone & Crockett points. It took me the rest of the day to get him out and back to our camp.

My brother, Doug, shot a black bear also that day with his .244 Remington.

We had a happy camp that night!

54

I shot this 27 inch muley buck on November 23 in Montana's Pryor Mountains. The Pryors don't have very many big bucks any more, due to too much hunting pressure on the bucks. Because of the good genetic there for big bucks, the area would be a prime candidate for a limited draw season for buck tags and management for high quality mule deer bucks. The following are some of the things about hunting big mule deer bucks I have learned through the years:

    • *When looking for elk or deer on a timbered hillside, from across a valley, you can see into the timber and can pick out a standing elk or deer as a horizontal line or a dark spot.*

    • *Wind blows down from a half hour after sunset to a half hour after sunrise, and up the rest of the time. You should hunt uphill as soon as you can see in the morning, because the air is still blowing down.*

    • *Big bucks bed on the north side of the hill in warm weather, but will bed at the head of a pocket in the sun during colder weather.*

    • *When big bucks are in rut, they travel at all times during the day or night.*

    • *A big buck usually makes a circle before bedding down so he can see or smell anything that follows him.*

I nailed this great 7x9 non-typical Muley on Sykes Ridge in the Pryor Mountains of Montana on November 24th. I miss most of my Thanksgiving dinners with family, due to hunting. Diana and I have a belated Thanksgiving dinner in December after hunting season closes. The time Diana and I spend apart due to my hunting makes us appreciate each other more. If people are in each other's company day in and day out, all year long, they tend to take the other person for granted and sometimes don't treat each other as good as they should. Absence makes the heart grow fonder and sometimes makes people realize the true value of the other partner. I think men should take their wives and families to the outdoors as much as they can. Most women don't care to go on the 20 below zero, windy, deer stands or the long, forced marches of a backpack sheep hunt. I think they are probably smarter than us "macho men". Besides hunting you can enjoy many other aspects of outdoor recreation with the family, such as picnics, fishing, hiking, bird watching, camping, butterfly and insect collection, tree and flower identification, or wildlife photography. Ease your family into reading about the outdoors. The subjects are many and varied, exciting and educational. Your family will understand you better also if they read and learn about your favorite sport.

Chapter 7

FUN IN THE SKY
OR SOMETIMES I'D RATHER WALK

Have you ever been somewhere that you didn't want to be. We have all been caught in these situations once in a while. Just up and leave, right? NOT!!

Small planes and me just don't seem to get along too well. I have been sick in petite aircraft so many times that the thought of an approaching plane ride used to make me nauseous. Some of these little planes also doubled as spray planes and I finally figured out that the retained chemicals on the plane were making me as sick as anything.

When I was guiding bighorn sheep hunters, I used to fly quite often to look for rams, and hopefully save a few hundred miles walking each fall, if I could just find which mountain that the sheep were on. Usually we didn't see rams from the air but if we did see sheep, it would be ewes and lambs. Only occasionally did we see rams. I have never been able to spot a ram from the air and go in and get it either with a guided hunter or for myself.

I learned most of what I know about sheep hunting in the Beartooth Mountains of Montana by trial and error through an awful lot of miles walked, cold camps endured, and vast terrain glassed.

I did learn the topography very well, from the Wyoming line to past the Boulder River. You study your maps beforehand and then when you fly over the area, it all comes together for you in your mind. I highly recommend this for anyone hunting any backcountry area. You discover things from the air that you can't see from the ground. I once discovered a snow slide that ran from near the top of the Fishtail Plateau almost to the road in the bottom of the canyon below. You couldn't see this cleared out swath from below. For years, I had fought my way up 4000 feet of elevation through thick, dog hair pine to hunt these upper reaches of bighorn sheep range. Now I climb the slide like it is a super highway.

I like to see the untamed country from the air, but after several years of being sloshed around while almost flying aerobatics when looking for sheep, I am close to developing an aversion to flying. I got so sick once that I actually thought for a split second, about opening the door and getting out until I remembered where I was.

An airline pilot once told me that a possible explanation for my air sickness was an over or well developed sense of balance. I don't know. I have noticed on normal flights where there isn't much violent tossing and turning or abrupt turns or turbulence, that I don't get sick. I don't get sick on large commercial airliners either. I'm sure some of the sickness is now a conditioned reflex from earlier abuses.

In 1976, I flew to the first Foundation for North American Wild Sheep (FNAWS) Convention in Des Moines, Iowa with a man that had killed a sheep with me the year before. I had flown commercially to Minneapolis, Minnesota from Billings, Montana and then flew from Minneapolis to Des Moines, Iowa with my friend. We stopped along the way and he traded for a newer plane, an amphibious model. He flew around for about an hour with the guy he traded with and received instructions on how to fly the new plane. I gladly stayed on the ground while this went on. After awhile my friend came back and picked me up, and we continued on toward Des Moines.

I looked at the gas gauge later that night and it read almost empty. I pointed this out to him and he said not to worry because we should be able to fly several more hours on the gas we had. I was not convinced and talked him into landing and spending the night at a small town with a little airport.

I watched in horror the next morning as the attendant put 40.2 gallons into the 40 gallon tank. We had been running on fumes the night before.

We finished our flight to Des Moines and we helped launch the Sheep Foundation that has grown to be such a force for, and stewardship of, North American big game animals since then.

I was active in the sheep foundation for several years and was once considered as a national director but due to other interests and a lack of time, declined the offer to run.

After the convention we started back toward Minneapolis and the same thing happened again. This time, while on the ground refueling, my friend asked another pilot some questions and discovered that he wasn't leaning his fuel control out once he was in flight and was thus using more gas than he thought he was. Two near crashes because of pilot error. I almost took the bus home from there. Really!

I tolerate small planes, because they are the only means of travel in many of the places I like to hunt, namely Alaska and parts of Canada.

My brother, Doug, is a bush pilot in Alaska and he is extremely competent. I would fly anywhere with him.

One bright, still fall day, I flew out of Red Lodge, Montana to look for bighorn sheep with a local pilot we will call Bob. Bob was a good pilot with a lot of spraying and mountain hours flown.

We were in a small two seater plane, equipped with a 150 horse engine, with the pilot in front and me seated behind. It was getting late in the year and there was some snow in the high country.

We had just flown across the alpine Silver Run Plateau and were headed toward the upper end of the rugged East Rosebud Canyon on our way to search for sheep between the West Rosebud and the Stillwater Rivers.

We were flying over some of the most rugged country in the Beartooths; sharp pinnacles, headwalls, cliffs, all of cold and brooding granite rock. I didn't even see any mountain goats in this sterile area.

I thought to myself that this would be a very bad place to go down in a crash. You probably couldn't even get down the snow covered cliffs to walk out.

Just as I was thinking about this sinister possibility, I heard a loud explosion. Bob stiffened in front of me and I came to quick attention also, bracing myself. The plane shuddered and we started to drop. The engine sputtered and began to run unevenly. Even with my inexperience with airplane engines, I knew something was wrong with the engine. Bob tipped the plane to the right and cleared a ridge by about 10 feet as we continued to drop out of the cold blue sky. After clearing the rocky ridge, we were headed down into a side canyon near the upper end of the East Rosebud drainage. We kept dropping and Bob fought to control the aircraft.

We now had a lot of air between us and the canyon floor because the canyon is very deep here. We flew, almost gliding, down the side canyon and swung right at the main canyon, and proceeded down it toward East Rosebud Lake.

The engine was a normally aspirated engine, not fuel injected or turbo charged. At high altitude, the less air the engine gets the less horsepower the engine has.

Bob was fighting for our survival. A crash here would probably be fatal. Bob had somewhat stabilized the plane, but we were still losing altitude, though not as fast now.

Bob yelled over his shoulder that he was going to try to make a belly landing on the rocky beach at East Rosebud Lake.

Remember about getting caught in places and situations where you didn't want to be? We were prisoners, possibly facing our own death. NEVER GIVE UP HOPE. SAY A PRAYER. IT'S NOT OVER UNTIL IT'S OVER.

We didn't drop as swiftly as Bob thought we would and when we came over East Rosebud Lake, we still had pretty good altitude, though I could see we were still slowly losing altitude.

Pretty quickly we had cleared the end of the canyon and swung to our right toward Red Lodge. We were now out over the open foothills and pastures and could probably make a safe forced landing if need be. The little plane's motor sputtered and ground along. I could see Red Lodge up ahead.

We were starting to get fairly close to the ground and I became nervous again as I watched ahead as we flew over a line of trees at treetop elevation. I could see the airport runway up ahead.

TIME FOR ANOTHER QUICK PRAYER.

Sometimes life hangs by a hair.

We cleared the barbed wire fence at the end of the runway by the narrowest of margins. It looked to me like we were going to hang a wheel in the top wire. Bob made a soft landing right at the end of the asphalt strip and we taxied to the hangar.

I got out of that man-made death trap as soon as I could and planted my feet on the terra firma. It sure felt good to be back where I, a land lover, belonged.

Bob raised the engine cover and there was a spark plug wire with a plug in it hanging down loose. After loss of the plug, we had lost 25% of our power on a 4 cylinder engine running at already reduced horsepower because of the altitude.

I reached up and felt the other plug and wire on that same cylinder. It was cold and came loose in my hand. If another plug would have come out also while we were flying, the engine would have quit and we would now be a smear on a rock face up the East Rosebud.

The mechanic had worked on the plane that morning and had forgotten to tighten the plugs. The mechanic said he could tighten them and Bob and I could go back out flying again. I told the mechanic what he could do with that idea real fast. I turned to Bob and congratulated him on his skill in keeping us flying, but told him that I thought that I had used up most of my flying luck for that day and would just go home instead.

I THANKED THE LORD FOR SAVING US THAT DAY.

I have known many pilots in the outdoor world who have been killed.

Jimmie Joe Ayling, the Hermit of the Beartooths, told me in 1966 that he didn't own or trust any kind of machine. He spoke specifically about manned space flights. He said sooner or later a machine would fail and people would die in space. The Challenger proved him right.

I don't trust machines either, but we live in an age where you couldn't keep up with the rest of the world without them.

I'd better grab my thesaurus, I don't think "fun" was quite the appropriate word I was searching for when I titled this piece.

I didn't fly again for quite some time.

Death rides a fast horse,
Don't look back,
Live every day as your last,
Death closes on your track.
Bill Butler, 1985

60

7x7 Mule Deer buck shot on the Stillwater River in the Beartooth Mountains of Montana. Outside spread 27-3/4 inches, gross Boone & Crockett non-typical score about 200 points, gross typical score 187 points. I spotted this big buck from a half a mile away with my spotting scope. I could see that he had deep forks, front and back. Depth of forks are noticeable even at long range. This buck was fairly heavy beamed and had four inch long brow points. Long brow points quickly add to a buck's total score. I stalked this buck to within 125 yards, just before sundown, and made an easy shot. I brought the buck back to the mountains the next day for a photo. These big bucks spend their summers in the high peaks and alpine areas grazing in the same meadows with bighorn sheep. Deep snows and the breeding season bring these old veterans down to the winter ranges. I was scouting for bighorn sheep when I killed this buck on November 14th. The ratio of big bucks to the total deer population is higher in backcountry mountainous areas. If you want to kill a real big trophy muley, take your backpack and hunt the high summering areas as soon as the season opens. Hunt them the same as you would hunt bighorn sheep, using a spotting scope to glass vast areas at and above timberline. Many high mountain hunting seasons don't open until late October. You are taking a chance going in then, because of early winter snowstorms, that could prove dangerous.

I knocked down this pretty 5x5 muley buck on the Custer National Forest in Montana on November 24, 1989. The buck was in heavy rut and was with about a dozen does at a water hole at first light. He ran up into the timber and stopped to look back, thinking he was concealed in the thick, dark timber. Here's where a good light gathering scope comes into play. I picked a clear path through the timber and shot the standing buck. My wife Diana was with me and I explained and demonstrated the basics of tracking to her as we followed the buck to where he went down from the lung shot. We had excellent eating from the buck's meat.

My efforts in 1991 were well rewarded when I harvested this 170 point 5x5 buck on November 20. There are still a few of these old ridge runners out there to hunt in Montana. If you really want a big mule deer buck, though, you should hunt Wyoming, Colorado, Utah, Arizona, Idaho or Nevada. There are two new video tapes on the market on mule deer. They are produced by Rod T. Eastman and are called "Extreme Bucks, Part I and II". They are the best tapes I have ever seen on super big, Boone & Crockett class muley bucks. For more information call 1-800-624-4311 or write R. T. Eastman Productions, P.O. Box 1531, Jackson Hole, Wyoming 83001.

December 17, 1966. The Pryor Mountains of Montana used to have a late mule deer season. One cold day a friend and I were hunting in a wide canyon at about 7500 feet elevation when I saw two large bucks walk into the timber about 400 yards up canyon from us. I mentally marked their last location, and climbed out of the canyon to the rim top. We circled ahead of where we thought the buck would be and sneaked over the rim for a look in an open area. One big buck was in the bottom of the canyon, starting up the far side. My friend shot and dropped the buck. I just caught a glimpse of the other buck as it ran into more timber on our left and up canyon. The rim top was fairly smooth and I got back away from the rim out of sight and sprinted for 100 yards to try to intercept the fleeing buck. As I peered over the rim again, there was the buck standing, looking back toward where the earlier shot had come from. The buck saw me and with much haste, charged down the hill, quartering off about 100 yards to my left. I was breathing very hard from the run at high altitude, but rapidly sat down, held my breath and shot. After the shot the buck ran 75 yards before falling and slid down hill another 30 feet. This was the first deer I ever had mounted.

Chapter 8

GOOD GRUB

The group of stubble-faced hunters crowded around the fire watching the boiling pot. I took a glove and removed the pot from the coals, poured the water off to reveal some cubes of meat in the bottom. Each man gingerly took out a chunk and stuck it, some very reluctantly, into their mouths. I chewed mine for a moment and quickly spat it out as did the others. We all began looking for mustard, catsup, gum, or anything else that would dispel the taste. This experiment happened a few years ago in a hunting camp in the Little Belt Mountains. We were trying coyote meat to see if it was edible. It very surely was not. It tasted musty and was so strong that you could not stand to have it in your mouth for more than a few seconds. It left a bad taste also.

I have tried eating many kinds of wild game through the years. Some are unexpectedly delicious, while others were like the coyote. I was raised on mule deer and antelope meat because my father is a good hunter and always had the deep freezer full. I cannot distinguish a difference in the taste of mule deer and whitetail. Whitetail meat is sometimes tighter grained probably because they are a more nervous animal and stay in better physical condition than mule deer do.

I like the taste of an antelope that has been stalked and shot without running it down. Any meat is better if it is properly cared for in the field. An animal should be field dressed first. Then scent glands can be removed later so that one does not get the musk on his hands, then all over the meat.

An animal should be cooled out quickly and kept cool. An old animal should be aged to tenderize it. I have aged old whitetail up to three weeks in cold weather. They should have the hide left on them and be hung in complete shade as the sun will rancid fat.

The taste of most meat is determined by what the animal eats. A moose killed early before the rut while it is still fat and feeding on grasses and sedges tastes much different from one that is killed late in the season and is thin from living on willows for awhile. High mountain grass fed deer, elk, moose, sheep and goat are all excellent eating with bighorn sheep my choice of all wild game. Mountain goats should be made into hamburger as most of them are too tough for steaks and chops.

I have eaten mountain lion and must say it is excellent with a taste like veal, tender, and light colored. One has to cook it well though because it sometimes contains trichinosis such as hogs have.

The bears, grizzly and black, also can have trichinosis and have to be cooked well. I have eaten both species of bear and do not like either. The meat is very greasy with a strong flavor. I could live on it if I had to. Marinating the meat in vinegar will make it taste much better (if you like vinegar).

I have eaten buffalo and like it also. It is somewhat like beef.

Javelina, from the southwest, is a small pig but the meat is lean and tastes somewhere between chicken and rabbit if properly cared for and prepared.

Bobcat tastes similar to rabbit. It has light colored meat but an old one is tough.

Porcupine should have all the fat removed and then boiled. It tastes something like turkey.

Wild animals live much cleaner than domestic ones, are leaner and usually eat less chemicals in their natural diet. A person can discover a whole new world of eating pleasure if he will realize that all his food doesn't have to come from a grocery store.

HUNTING TIPS:

Always go directly to where you last saw an animal that you shot at and look for cut hair, blood, fat, viscera, or bone.

Lung blood is bright red, muscle blood is dark red and doesn't bleed as heavily as a lung shot unless an artery has been hit.

You may not find blood immediately. An animal may run 100 yards before starting to bleed.

Track the buck out for three hundred yards and if you cannot find any sign of a hit, then and only then, can you assume that you didn't hit the animal. Also make sure that you have the right tracks.

A wounded animal will sometimes leave an unnatural track as a leg dangles or sticks out at an odd direction.

A lantern is very good to use at night to follow wounded game because the blood shows shiny in the light.

Wild birds such as magpies, crows, ravens, Clarks nutcrackers, and eagles have good eyes. They don't miss anything and will quickly locate downed, wounded or dead game animals, looking for a free meal. They can sometimes lead you to your downed trophy.

Chapter 9

RUMOR TO REALITY -THE SEARCH FOR RECORD PRONGHORN

Reprinted with permission of Petersen's Hunting Magazine

I could see the light colored pickup approaching quickly in the rear view mirror. From where I sat in my Ford pickup glassing the surrounding prairie and rolling hills, I could see several small herds of antelope. There weren't any good bucks in any of the herds. It was the day before opening day of antelope season in eastern Montana.

The pickup pulled to a stop along side mine on the dusty ranch road. There were a man and a woman in the vehicle and the man asked "Seen anything?".

"No, not anything of any quality, I've seen plenty of bucks but no real big ones," I said.

"You're just hunting a big one, huh?" he returned. "We got a 15-1/2 incher out of here last year." Then abruptly he asked, "Do you have permission to be in here?"

"Yea, I do," I said. "I know Joe, I check this ranch every year, I hunt several ranches in this area." At the mention of the rancher's name, the man relaxed again and talked more freely.

They told me; where they were camped, where they lived 400 miles west of here, how they had seen a red fox, and how she had photographed a large 6 x 6 whitetail in a small draw up from the valley in the edge of the hills. They also told me about seeing an extremely large antelope buck to the north of the highway about seven more miles west from this ranch. They said they had seen it the day before as they were arriving into the area. To the north of the road was not in their permit area or mine either for that matter.

I thought they might be lying to me to get rid of me. If they were, why would they tell me about a big buck that was not in my area either.

I asked them and they told me the exact mile post number on the highway and that there was a reservoir about four hundred yards off the road to the north. I thanked them, wished them luck, turned around and drove back to the main highway. I quickly and anxiously drove the seven miles west to the mile post sign they had mentioned.

I stopped on the side of the road and started to glass out the rider's side of the pickup to the north. I saw the earthen dam of the reservoir that they talked about. There were two small buck antelope here, standing watching me. I glassed the large basin, dissecting it with my spotting scope, minutely and thoroughly.

I thought if I found the large buck, maybe I could watch it, and maybe it would cross into my area where I could hunt it the next day. He was no where to be found though. The fence on either side of the road was sheep tight and probably antelope tight also. Not many antelope jump fences, but crawl through them. The antelope couldn't crawl through this one as far as I could tell.

While I was here I thought I might as well scour the area to the south of the road also, just in case the buck had somehow crossed the road. I started to glass the flat valley with a windmill at one end of it. Soon I picked up antelope coming out of a deep cut in the middle of the valley and heading toward the windmill for their evening drink. There were several does strung out in single file walking toward the water. I looked on to the left, from where the antelope had come and there suddenly was a large buck, broadside, walking in my Bausch and Lomb field of view. Sun reflected off of his long black horns and he slowly walked after the does and toward the water. His horns looked longer than any I had ever seen on a live antelope in Montana. I watched him until he drank and went back to feeding. This may have been the same buck that the other hunters had seen across the road out of my legal area. How ever he got here, he was now in my area.

I drove back the way I had come to an access road that led into a set of ranch buildings. The rancher was harvesting alfalfa seed with a combine. I walked out to him and asked permission to hunt. He said that I could hunt but that he only had about 60 antelope on his land.

I was at the ranch the next morning before daylight. The morning was clear and cool, typical of Montana's October.

Two other men were the only other hunters with permission to hunt on the property.

I usually drive hundreds of miles while scouting. I drive every road there is on a ranch and walk to the areas of the ranches that I can't see from the small ranch roads. Don't ever drive off the ranch roads because most ranchers disapprove of this practice. You break over grass that cattle eat and also you make ruts that start erosion. Although I drive an extreme amount while scouting, I always hunt on foot.

Trophy hunting is a matter of percentages. You have to cover a lot of country and look at a lot of animals, usually, before you find a buck that you think is record class. If you will be satisfied with an average buck, then you can probably get it on the first ranch you hunt. I usually hunt several ranches before I find a buck I think will make the record books.

I walked along under a ridge crest and located a fairly good sized herd of antelope out in a big flat about 500 yards from me. The big buck was

82-2/8 point Antelope Buck

with them but because of the flatness, I was unable to approach them. The other hunters showed up. They had not seen me, and attempted a stalk, which frightened the antelope over a small pass near three buttes. One hunter took a long shot at the running antelope.

I followed the antelope over the ridge on foot and made two stalks on them but they were spooked now and were gone when I got to where they had been. The antelope went through the pass near the three buttes twice more as they would see the the other hunters at long range and move away. The second time I located the buck was at 800 yards where he climbed one of the three conical buttes and stood watching in all directions for 40 minutes. He had nine does and a small buck with him, a lot of eyes for me to contend with. He was gone when I got there.

I use the contour of the land when I stalk a pronghorn buck. There are usually ravines that cut the prairie and most are deep enough to walk or crawl in to approach a buck unseen. I also use ridges and rolling terrain wherever possible. I once stalked down the opposite side of a barbed wire fence from a buck. The buck was close to the fence and at the angle that I was from him, the wooden posts all ran together and because of us both being close to the fence but on opposite sides, the buck could not see me because of the alignment of the posts. I was guiding at the time and worked my hunter to an easy shot within 150 yards of the feeding buck with nothing more than a wire fence for cover.

Back to my original story, I hoped the other hunters would get their antelope soon, so that the antelope would settle down and I could successfully stalk the buck.

I decided that since the large buck had already gone through the pass three times that morning, he probably would again. I hid myself among the blue gumbo buttes and waited.

Soon a hunter appeared about three fourths of a mile away. The herd of antelope on the flat started to drift slowly up the hill toward me. They were extremely spooky now and were moving at the first sight of a man.

I laid low on the shoulder of one of the buttes and watched the wary animals approach. An alert eyed, young buck and ten does passed by at 200 yards. I never twitched a muscle. Then the large buck showed up, walking in the midst of several does. I followed him in my scope with the safety off, ready to shoot. He was clear for an instant but not long enough for a shot. Then quickly another chance presented itself. The buck was walking slowly with no other antelope near him. I shot and hit him high in the lungs, heard the impact of the bullet, and then regained my sight picture after the recoil, to see him down.

I walked down to him and the closer I got the bigger he looked. A magnificent buck, he was very large and beautiful. He was thin with age, but not too thin. He had the brown nose of an old buck. The tape on his horn said he was 17 inches long. After drying for 60 days, the trophy scored 82-2/8 Boone & Crockett points officially.

The other hunters got their antelope also, and went home. Sometimes when other hunters are moving the antelope around, you are better off to just sit still and let them move a buck to you.

This buck had started out as a rumor and now was a reality. Don't hesitate to check out a buck that someone tells you about.

This Antelope buck green scored 81 points.

Another example of checking out stories happened in the fall of 1985. After hunting several days and several ranches, I stopped in and asked a new rancher to hunt. He had most of the ranch leased to an outfitter but said I could hunt a six section pasture he owned to the north. A section is 640 acres and is a mile on each side. This is a relatively small place to hunt compared to some of the ranches I have hunted antelope on. One ranch that I had previously hunted on had 350 sections and another had 175 sections.

I asked the rancher, as I always do, if he knew about any large bucks in the six section pasture. He said there was one, a very heavy horned buck with nice prongs and fairly long horns.

The rancher rode out with me to show me the boundaries so that I would not get in the wrong pasture or on a neighbor's land. The lay of the land was extremely rough for antelope habitat.

We rode all of the roads in the pasture, but didn't see the buck. He said he figured the buck was in the pasture somewhere so I spent the next several hours on foot, searching out every nook and cranny in the jumbled terrain.

When I finally saw the buck, he was running in the middle of a herd at 300 yards. The antelope had seen me first. The buck's horns stood out, even at that distance. They looked extremely black and large, like black 2x4 blocks sticking out of his head.

They ran to a far hill and stopped to graze. It had rained recently, and my stalk up a gully led me through thigh deep water. I had to stay in the water to stay out of sight of the herd. It was the only way I had to stalk the buck. I was only able to approach to within 300 yards of the herd. I found a good rest for my rifle and killed the buck from my hidden position. My water filled boots sloshed along on the dry prairie as I walked up to the elusive buck.

The buck had 15-1/2 inch horns, 7 inch bases and long prongs. He green scored 81 points.

Through 1989, I had taken seventeen bucks that made Safari Club International's minimum score of 70 points. Many of these scored close to 80 points and two scored over the all time Boone & Crockett minimum of 82 points. The antelope buck that I shot in the fall of 1989 had 8-3/8" bases, and scored an official 86 Boone & Crockett points. This buck is the fourth largest antelope that has ever been taken in Montana, but that is a whole other story.

Killing just any antelope can be extremely easy, but to consistently take extra large old bucks requires time, patience, persistence, hard work, dedication, and sometimes running down rumors.

I was in the Denver Museum of Natural History once, and saw there a skeleton of a 4-horned antelope that existed in North America, 25,000 years ago. This recessive trait surfaces occasionally in modern antelope. I took this fine buck on October 14th in Garfield County, Montana. It scored 77 points in SCI Record Book and has 1-1/2 inch horns growing independently behind each of the main horns. The buck was grazing by himself on top of a hill in knee high grass. There was a wire fence running across the hill between me and the buck. I lined up behind one of the posts and crawled when the buck's head was down in the grass as he fed. One hundred yard standing shots are a "piece of cake".

(Photo first appeared in Mike Eastman's Outdoor Journal, Vol. 5, Issue 19, 1992)
I shot this whopper of an antelope in Natrona County, Wyoming on September 19, 1992. It field dressed 103 lbs., had 16-1/4 inch long horns with 5-1/4 inch prongs. It makes Boone & Crockett Awards Book with the official score of 80-6/8 points. The area where I got the buck had historically produced Boone & Crockett antelope, but at the present time was not known for its trophies. I hiked into an extremely rough, roadless area that also had mule deer and elk. There was a good herd of antelope living in the steep, rocky, partly timbered area. I studied the buck for four hours before shooting it. Because of the buck's body size and unusual confirmation of its horns, he was tough to judge.

(Photo first appeared in Mike Eastman's Outdoor Journal, Vol. 5, Issue 19, 1992)
I was hunting on one of Montana's Block Management ranches that allows only walk-in hunting, when I shot this 15-1/2 inch antelope buck with a 6-5/8 inch prong, on October 13, 1992. The buck weighed 77 lbs. field dressed. The official Boone & Crockett score is 83-6/8 points. My fourth Boone & Crockett antelope to date. I started walking early and saw some antelope. The further I got from the main road the more antelope I saw. When I had travelled to the most distant area of the ranch, I spotted a 78 point buck. With a little more looking, I found this bruiser. After a half mile stalk and a 100 yard shot, the giant was mine. I find trophy antelope hunting extremely enjoyable and rewarding.

Mountain Lion taken in the Beartooth Mountains of Montana on a snowy, cold January day. This tom weighed 156 pounds and scored 14-6/16 SCI. With the aid of a friend and his 11 year old black and tan hound, named "Puppy", and one shot from a single shot 22 rifle, I was able to bring this trophy home. I have the mountain lion life-size mounted now. This was the last of the Montana Big Ten that I had been searching for. Due to controlled hunting, the mountain lion population is very high in the western United States, and is in no way endangered. I have owned trail hounds off and on all my life and presently have two treeing walker hounds.

I photographed this bighorn ram on the winter range in January 1988 near Anaconda, Montana. The ram, later taken by Lester Kish, was the largest Boone & Crockett ram ever taken by a hunter south of Canada scoring 200-7/8 B&C, with a horn length of 49-2/8".

Chapter 10

CHECKLIST FOR BACKPACK HUNTING

EQUIPMENT:

1.   Large backpack with two main pockets, the upper one opens from the top. The backpack should have many pockets so you don't have to dig to the bottom every time you want something. Have a place for everything, and everything in its place. The zippers on the small pockets should be on top for easy access when the pack is lying flat on its shoulder straps. Shoulder straps should be well padded. I like an adjustable waist belt also. Backpack should have external frame because an internal frame type will not carry a real heavy load without hurting you. The pack should stand by itself, in case you take it off in rain or snow, and also a standing pack is easier to get onto your shoulders when it is loaded heavily. Carry a couple of extra pins to hook the pack to the frame in case you lose one. I take my pack in the tent at night so it will be out of the weather and away from animals.

2.   Small day pack for hunting after you get there. I like two large pockets so you can get at things easier. It should be tear-drop shaped so it doesn't catch on brush, etc. as you hunt. It should have well padded shoulder straps. It should be big enough to hold your rain jacket, space blanket, extra shells, lunch, sharpening stone, first aid kit, toilet paper, gloves, flashlight, moleskin, camera, etc. Sometimes, if I am carrying a heavy load of meat out, I put my day pack on backwards with it on the front of my body to counterbalance my load. I personally do not like fanny packs because; you sweat too much under them, they hold your coat away from you in cold weather, they don't hold enough gear, and they also cut off circulation to your legs, because you have to tighten them extremely tight so they don't slip down with a heavy load, thus weakening your legs quicker.

3.   Tent with a floor, rain fly, poles, stakes. A four season tent with extra poles is best to hold up in a heavy snowstorm or high winds. I have had good experience with dome tents in extremely bad weather.

4.   Quallofil sleeping bag and stuff bag (Quallofil will stay warm when wet). My personal sleeping bag is good to -20 degrees Fahrenheit.

5.   Air mattress or pad. Thermarest 3/4 length. You don't need support past your knees.

6.   Rifle and extra shells. I shoot 180 grain bullets because they carry better in high winds, thus making them more accurate. (Optional) Cleaning kit.

7.   Good compass - don't skimp here because it might save your life. I use a Silva compass.

8.   Flashlight - Mini-Maglite and extra Duracell batteries.

9.   Camera and extra rolls of film. Optional - lens cleaner, fill in flash, telephoto lens.

10. Hunting knife. I use a Gerber folding pocket knife.

11. Spotting scope and small tripod, tripod should work on camera also. I have a 15 to 60 variable power.

12. Small binoculars - I use Zeiss 10x25 power.

13. Toilet paper.

14. Maps of area. I use the most current, detailed topographical maps I can obtain.

15. Space blanket - the larger, better ones.

16. Stone or steel for sharpening hunting knife (don't carry both).

17. Fluorescent orange clothing if required in your state.

18. Light nylon cord 20 feet, it has many uses. To tie a cape or head onto a pack, to hang meat, replace a shoelace, or general repairs.

19. Sportsman saw to cut out horns, etc.

20. Garbage bags (heavy duty) for meat. Cool meat first before sealing in bags. Take the meat out of the plastic bags and hang it in the shade if stopping for long periods of time in warm weather. Get meat out of the backcountry as quick as possible.

21. Salt for capes if you are going to be in the mountains quite awhile.

22. Fluorescent flagging tape to help you find a kill site easier.

23. Soap - small and plastic ziploc bag to hold it.

24. Towel - small.

25. Radio (optional) for weather reports or hunting reports. I put the radio right against my ear on low volume so that I don't spook game that might be in the area.

26. Fishing gear (optional) to catch extra food.

27. Wristwatch with thermometer and altimeter. I have a Casio.

28. Sunglasses (optional).

CLOTHING:

1.   Insulated leather boots (for non-snow conditions) - I use Danner Osprey for two reasons, a) I get better grip with the air-bob soles, and b) the laces go further down the toe than other boots do, allowing you to tighten up the slack in the toe area to prevent blisters.

2.   Cabela's Expedition Pac Boot by Sorel. Guaranteed to 85 degrees below 0 Fahrenheit. My feet tend to get cold, but they haven't been cold in this boot. These also have air-bob soles.

3.   Jackets. I use a heavy wool jacket (King-of-The-Mountain camouflage) until it gets real cold, then I use a down jacket. I use a heavy thigh-length hooded down jacket to hunt in extremely cold weather. I used it once elk hunting at -22 degrees Fahrenheit.

4.   Wool pants-these are very important. They will stay warm even when wet. They could save your life. I use King-of-The-Mountain because they have a terrific camouflage pattern.

5.   Wool shirt, or if wool bothers you close to your skin, wear as I do, Cabela's Worsterlon Outdoorsman shirt. This is a warm and rugged shirt. The Brown Camo Pattern blends well in the terrain I hunt.

6.   Thermax or polypropylene long sleeve t-shirt and briefs.

7.   Long underwear, tops and bottoms, polypropylene or Thermax inner-wool outer.

8.   Warm cap with warm ear flaps. Wool (outer) and polypropylene (inner) balaclava or face mask. Light baseball cap for warm days.

9.   Rain jacket - high quality advised. I use Cabela's ambush cloth Goretex rainwear in uninsulated Brown Camo Pattern.

10.   Winter leather mittens with fingered wool inner liners are my choice because mittens are warmer than just fingered gloves.

11.   Wool socks (2) pair. They should contain some synthetic which makes them wear longer.

12.   Polypropylene socks (2) pair (they wick moisture away from your feet and keep them dry and warmer).

FIRST AID KIT:

1.   Antiseptic - New Skin for cuts, abrasions, etc.

2.   Vaseline for chapped skin. Legs may become raw where they are rubbed by wool pants.

3.   Band-aids (10-15) for blisters, etc.

4.   Moleskin for feet, to prevent blisters.

5.   Elastic bandage for sprains.

6.   Pepto Bismal tablets (they can save a trip).

7.   1" wide adhesive tape.

8.   Salt tablets or potassium. As soon as you stop to make camp, take one of these to prevent muscle cramps from occurring later in the night, especially the first night out when muscles are still unaccustomed to the exertion.

9.   Suntan lotion - sweatproof, SPF 15 (or greater) sunblock. Summer and early fall, especially at high altitudes because the atmosphere is thinner and you burn more easily.

10.   Aspirin.

11. Vitamins (multiple with minerals).

12. Tweezers for cactus, slivers, etc.

13. Water purification device, otherwise you have to boil water to kill giardia flagellates. Water purification pills have failed me in the past and I got giardiasis.

14. Toothbrush and small toothpaste.

FOOD:

You can buy most of what you need in a regular grocery store. Look for things that are nutritious yet light to carry.

1. Black tea bags
    Instant Noodle Dishes - Top Ramen, fettuccine, etc.
    Potato buds
    Dehydrated milk
    Instant breakfast
    Instant oatmeal
    Cup-o-soup
    Mountain House (brand): beef stew, chicken stew, pork chops, beef patties or pieces
    Granola bars
    Hot chocolate
    Pepper/salt
    Candy bars
    Dried fruit
    Jerky
    Squeeze cheese snacks - the kind that do not require refrigeration
    Crackers

Remove foods from bulky packaging and repackage in ziploc, etc., so they will take less space in your pack.

2. Plastic mixing container (wide top) for Gatorade.

3. Scotch brite pad (to keep kettles clean).

4. Spoon and metal sierra cup.

5. Kettle and lid.

6. Mountain Safety Research gas stove and extra fuel.

7. Many wooden matches and waterproof container. I also carry a Bic lighter for convenience.

BACKPACKING ADVICE:

This list is basically what I use to hunt in the fall. Over 28 years of backpacking experience has gone into the selection of this list. I try to use what I think is the very best equipment, because my life has depended on my gear many times. Utilizing the best equipment makes the experience much more pleasant and good gear will last much longer than a cheaper brand. I upgrade my gear as new technology shows me a better way or as I can afford it.

Your list will vary according to your own particular hunting area, personal needs and tastes.

You probably won't be able to carry all of this, and it is safer to hunt with a partner anyway and split the weight with them. There are many common items used by both of you. If you go alone, you might consider a llama to pack some of your gear. I hunt alone a lot of the time, but I have to carry an extremely heavy pack.

If you are packing out meat and can't carry your camp out at the same time, take your meat out first and come back for your camp later. You may get a late start coming back for your camp and have to spend an extra, unplanned night at your camp. If you had taken your camp out first and then came back for your meat last, there is the possibility of getting caught in bad weather, running out of daylight, or getting hurt. If any of these things happen, you would need your camp to shelter you.

I strongly suggest that you start your backpacking in the summer in moderate weather because if you make a mistake then, it may not prove as critical or life threatening as it might in colder weather.

I recommend starting with just day trips or overnight trips and light packs until you become more proficient at backpacking.

New Skin antiseptic available from:
Medtech Laboratories, Inc.
P.O. Box 1108, 3510 North Lake Creek Drive
Jackson, Wyoming 83001
1-800-443-4908

King of the Mountain Camouflage Wool Clothing available from:
King of the Mountain
2709 West Eisenhower
Loveland, Colorado 80537
(303) 962-9306

Chapter 11

BACKPACK SHEEP HUNT
(Our First Major Backcountry Backpack Hunt)

In the mellow sun of a late October evening, my brother Doug and I sat on a shoulder of Mount Wood glassing for bighorn sheep. We were a short way from the summit of Montana's second highest peak as we peered over the brink of a headwall that dropped away, over a thousand feet, to an emerald lake and the upper reaches of Chicken Creek. Below us across the canyon was Pyramid Mountain and the Fishtail Plateau.

We were thoroughly searching every crevice and moraine pile with our 15 to 60 power Bausch and Lomb spotting scopes for the chocolate bodied, white-rumped bighorn rams. About a mile below us we had already spotted three ewes in a jumble of boulders bigger than trucks.

We had left the Mystic Lake power plant about a week before and had seen sheep every day — ewes and lambs and immature rams — but nothing with a legal 3/4 curl.

I had glassed all the area below us in the canyon and had just started to glass the plateau on the other side with the scope set on 15 power. I immediately spotted two rams, one on a grassy hillside with its rump to us and another above it as it walked toward us out of a small depression in the gently sloping tundra.

These sheep were a good two miles away, but with the scope on 15 power were easily recognizable as rams. I flipped the scope to 60 power, removed my hand from the tripod, and held my breath as I looked at the lower ram, a 7/8 curl. Then I shifted the scope to the upper ram, an old timer with heavily broomed, tightly curling horns that came back up a long ways. Doug and I watched the rams until dark, marking their positions on a topographical map. They were just brown specks to the naked eye.

The next day we got up early, ate, loaded our packs, and headed up a ridge and across a glacier to the summit of Mount Wood which has an elevation of 12,661 feet. From here a person can see much of Montana.

The night before we had looked at the weather tower sixty miles away on a Billings bank, with a spotting scope, and it indicated that there was a storm coming. If colder weather was moving in, we didn't want to have to go back the way we had come. But we knew that we might have to because we were not sure we could cross from Mount Wood to the

Fishtail Plateau where we had spotted the rams. There was a narrow ridge of bare rock connecting the mountain and plateau as it was shown on our topographical maps.

We started across the narrow ridge and the going was rough over big boulders and down small precipices. One place we had to hang down by our hands over a cliff and drop several feet to the ground below.

We figured we could go back up the escarpment if we had to turn back because of a larger dropoff further on. We didn't encounter anymore obstacles to stop our journey.

We reached a point about dark where we could see the hillside where the rams had been. The smaller ram was grazing at about 600 yards. The big ram was not in sight.

We could have stalked within 200 yards and killed the 7/8 curl ram about as the last light left the sky. Instead we decided to wait until morning and try to get both instead of shooting one and spooking the other.

Doug and I camped there that night and were awakened by the sound of snowflakes falling on our nylon tent the next morning. We loaded up camp without even eating and went to search for the big rams as a blizzard descended on the mountain.

Where we had seen sheep the night before, there were none. Nothing alive showed on the mountains above timber line. The sheep had all moved down into the timber to avoid the storm. The storm increased in intensity and we were forced to reluctantly leave the mountain.

Nobody said that getting a bighorn ram was an easy job, but as determined sheep hunters, the light of destiny was to shine more favorably on us later in the season as we both killed rams on the same day several miles apart in different drainages, me watching Doug make a long stalk, then him watching while I stalked a different ram close enough for a shot.

I had seen the bigger ram on the winter range after the season in 1967. We failed to kill him in 1968. This ram was killed by another hunter in mid-September 1969, and scored 181-1/8 Boone & Crockett points. He's listed in the all-time Boone & Crockett book.

"This day is mine to delight in. Success, happiness, excited anticipation. God, please give me guidance, an open mind to receive it, and the fortitude to act upon it."

Bill Butler
9-30-86

Chapter 12

WIDEWATER MOOSE

The day was fairly sunny and clear as we shouldered our backpacks and started out up the trail. It was September 16, the second day of the moose season, and I had drawn a permit for area 515. Area 515 lies in the southwest corner of Carbon County near Cooke City, Montana.

A friend was with me on the hunt. He is an airline pilot, who spends all his free time in the summer backpacking and fishing the Beartooth Mountains. We were headed for Widewater Lake to set up our base camp to hunt out of in all directions. Upstream from Widewater Lake is Fox Lake of which only the lower end is in area 515. Downstream is Big Moose Lake of which only the upper end is in hunting area 515.

There are big swampy areas between the lakes where the moose like to feed. A hunter must have good maps and know how to read them if he wants to stay in his legal hunting area. We left the vehicles at the foot bridge crossing on the Clarks Fork and walked past Kersey Lake to the Beartooth Primitive Area boundary. Here, we turned towards Rock Island Lake and walked past it to Fox Lake and on until we were near the upper end of Widewater Lake. At this point, we left the trail and headed out cross country for maybe half a mile until we came out on the edge of the glimmering Widewater Lake. I had been in the area fishing about a month before and had seen a small bull moose on the west side of Fox Lake. The pilot had seen a large bull on Russell Creek also about the same time. I had outfitted the area with hunters in past years and had seen some big bulls. I knew the area contained some good bulls then. After coming out on the edge of Widewater Lake, we walked over to where the stream from Fox Lake runs into Widewater Lake. We knew there was a good camping area there. We had seen fresh moose tracks along the lake as we followed its edge to the camping area.

We threw our packs off, admired the view a few moments and then the pilot started to set up camp. I grabbed my 30.06 and was going to have a look around before dark. I started up the stream and before I had gone 25 yards in the thick brush along the edge, I stopped. I could not believe what I saw. There on the other side of the stream where it empties into the lake was a big bull moose. The moose stood and looked at me. I yelled for the pilot to come and look at what I had found. He came after awhile and I asked him what he thought. He said, "He looks big to me." I looked at the bull a long time before I decided to shoot. The bull finally decided he had seen enough of us and started off up along the far creek

Trophy Bull Shiras Moose

bank. I shot from a standing offhand position but after one shot the bull fell at the edge of the water, hit in the spine.

We dressed the moose, went back to town, rented horses and packed out the moose the next few days. The moose weighed approximately 950 pounds live weight. The bull had a 45 inch spread with 6 points on each side, big enough for my first moose. It qualifies for Safari Club International's Record Book. I had always wanted a trophy moose, now I had one.

Bull Moose near Widewater Lake.

HUNTING TIPS:

If a moose knows you are on its track, it can be as difficult to get a look at as a bull elk. Otherwise moose are not difficult to hunt.

Game animals are more wary when they first come out in the evening, than they are right at dawn—after they have been up and around all night and are aware of most of the danger nearby.

Look back often. When you're hiking in strange country, if you look back regularly, you will be able to find your way back more easily. You will also see game that you passed by unnoticed, but are now looking out of their hiding place at you.

Chapter 13

PRE-SEASON SCOUTING

There is a change taking place. It's hard to see, but can be seen if one looks. Summer is fading into fall. The grass on the hills is cured, standing brittle, dry and brown. The days are getting shorter, the heat of the day cools quicker in the evenings and is slower to warm in the morning. The summer haze in the sky is clearing gradually to the gin-clear brightness of fall. The apples and berries are ripening and game animals, furbearers, and birds are getting the coats they will wear till spring.

The horns of the whitetail and mule deer, elk, moose, and antelope are full grown. If a person is interested in taking a trophy big game animal this fall, now is the time to seek it out. Some real good trophies are happened onto accidentally. To take them consistently; however, one must find the animal and watch him to try to learn his living habits and patterns now in the late summer, while he is still fairly docile and serene, before the shooting starts.

On the first day of hunting season, game animals will be fairly quiet and still unless you have wandered too close to them or have disturbed them some other way, such as setting up a hunting camp in their immediate habitat. Too many people using an area, sighting in rifles, talking, banging pots, pans, and car doors, will alert game to the forthcoming season. Some animals such as old bucks, elk, moose or sheep may move back into the mountains several miles from where you have watched them in the summer because of the disturbance.

When forced to hunt near a road, always try to walk at least a mile away from the road to do your hunting. This is the maximum distance most people will walk, and the game stays pushed back beyond this parameter.

The thing to do is to go to the backcountry, away from where all the people will be, and find a good trophy. The old mossbacks will usually be back there anyway. When you find a trophy animal in the backcountry, don't disturb him. Watch him from long distances with a spotting scope and don't let him see you if you can help it. Don't ride or walk through his area any more than is absolutely necessary. After you once find the animal, watch him for a couple of days to make sure he is staying in that general area. Then go, leave him alone. If you stay too long he will see you or otherwise become aware of you and may change areas.

If the animal has spent the summer there, as he probably has, then he should be close to the same area when hunting season opens, unless snow drives him down towards his wintering area. Be sure to get back in the area as soon as the season opens to hunt.

I kept tabs on this big buck throughout late summer and early fall. Then when hunting season came around I was busy with guiding hunters in another area and didn't get a chance to hunt the buck until late in the season, taking him on November 5 the last day of the season in that area. I walked up on the nice buck in a juniper pocket just after sunrise. The buck with a herd of does hadn't bedded yet and the whole herd spooked with the 6x6 buck following at a long legged trot. I broke the buck's back with an offhand shot at 125 yards. The buck was the biggest mule deer that I ever took in the local area where I was raised. Summer is a good time to scout and get permission to hunt. If you ask permission in the summer or early fall before all the other hunters start bothering the ranchers, you have a better chance of getting permission. The game is much less wary then also, and you have more time to size up heads. If you can find a good buck in the preseason, then you can more easily pass up smaller animals and hold out for the trophy that you already know exists. Mule deer bucks band up in the summer with as many as 30 to a bunch in high mountain summering areas.

Chapter 14

A BIG BUCK FOR DAD

I had been in the deep side canyon in the Beartooth Mountains, earlier in the fall. My purpose at that time was to find a bighorn ram for a hunter who would arrive shortly. It was normally too early to find rams there. However, I had seen them there early in the fall on occasion in the past. I thought the time would be well spent to take a look now. The fall was a clear, open one without much snow so far.

With my spotting scope, I thoroughly dissected the open canyon for any sign of a bighorn ram. Sheep there weren't, but deer there were. Only they were all does. I saw about a dozen mule deer does feeding near the patch of mature timber in the bottom of the canyon. In this high alpine sheep country, it was unusual to see so many does together. I see mule deer often in sheep country, but usually only a few at a time. It was about mid-October. I made myself a promise to return toward mid-November to see how big the mature buck would be that would join them from some hidden spot of summer seclusion. I forgot about the does for a while as I went about my guiding chores.

About the tenth of November, I stopped by my parents' place for a visit. My dad was a postmaster and ran a country store. My mother was a school teacher and homemaker. Our talk soon turned to hunting with questions about how the guiding was going. I informed them that my hunters had taken bighorn sheep, mule deer and elk so far.

My father had been mostly a meat hunter that had raised a family off the bounty of the Montana land. He had taken a big antelope once with a spectacular shot. He was an excellent shot at still or running game and was proud of that ability. He once won an NRA Bigbore Shoot that was held locally. He had also taken a bull elk and many mule deer, both bucks and does, but never a real big buck. His bag also included many antelope.

He had started me hunting early on with a BB gun and then with a .22 single shot Stevens rifle before I was 10 years old. The rifle was a birthday present for my brother, Jim, and I.

Dad had had a chance to shoot a black bear once, but had let me shoot it instead. I was 14 years old at the time. Also, my dad, Jim, was with me when I shot my first deer in 1958 when I was 12. My brothers, Doug and Jim, were along but were too young to hunt yet. My grandfather on my mother's side was also with us.

We were at the edge of a precipice at dawn, watching down into a large, open, sage covered valley. We had spotted a herd of several mule deer coming up towards us. They had been spooked out of the bottom

93

My first buck, a 5x5 Mule Deer.

by some other hunters. As the deer got closer, we could see the last one was a mature buck. A 5x5 with a big body. The deer came up onto a bench located just below our position and crossed single file through a sagebrush flat about 100 yards below us, running from left to right.

I got so excited, my first case of buck fever, that I ejected all of my shells from my 30.30 Winchester. I tried to shoot but couldn't. Looking at the ground, I saw all of my shells there. While I was doing this my grandfather and father were shooting. My dad broke a hind leg on the buck just above the hock with his first shot. Before my dad could shoot again, I had reloaded my rifle and put a lucky round through the buck's shoulders. My grandfather had missed. My dad had me tag the 5x5 buck, in my mind a virtual giant.

Growing up through high school, my brothers and I hunted as intensely as young wolves, taking many deer and antelope. Soon we were shooting the legal limit of two deer each. We had more than enough meat to eat at home and supplied several neighbors also.

My dad could see no good reason to hunt anymore, with his boys securing such an abundance of game, so he turned more to his greater love, fishing.

At the time we were talking, in dad and mother's kitchen, he had not shot a rifle at a game animal in 10 years. Dad had sold his rifle to me, a Husqvarna Crown Grade 30-06. I use it to this day. He said he had always wanted to shoot a big muley buck but didn't think he ever would now. I immediately thought of the herd of mule deer does and thought there was a good chance that a big buck would be with them by now.

It was early afternoon and I told my dad about the does and that I thought that we might find a big buck with them. The area was fairly close to a road and it wouldn't be very difficult to go take a look. We gathered our gear, and after buying him a license, were headed up the mountain.

I had shot a lot of big bucks and would let him do all the shooting today.

Remembering his habit of shooting the first buck he saw, I said, "I don't want you shooting any little two pointer today". He snapped back, "Well, I don't have to shoot a big six pointer".

We traveled up to over 10,000 feet elevation on the mellow Indian summer day. We parked the pickup and walked across the rocky alpine plateau to the edge of the deeply glaciated canyon. There wasn't any cover to mask us as we peeked over the edge, into the deep chasm below. I looked first to the exact spot where I had seen the does in October. I immediately saw a doe feeding in a brushy pocket and then saw another laying down looking directly at us from a grassy hump at the end of a finger of brush. We had silhouetted ourselves, but there was no other way to do things any differently.

By now, the sun was about to set and the canyon was already darkening quickly because of the sun's low angle behind us. The doe became more suspicious by the second, and sprang to her feet, staring directly at us up the hill. Just then, a large, super wild mule deer buck dashed out from behind the finger of brush and stood with one front leg raised, snapping his head from side to side looking for what had spooked the doe. The buck dashed back and forth a couple of times intently looking for the danger.

95

My dad's first big buck.

I was watching the buck with my spotting scope and told my dad that the buck was a good one. My dad had the 30.06 to his shoulder, and from his sitting position, was looking in the general direction of the deer. He had been able to see the deer with his naked eye but couldn't see it in his scope and told me so in a whisper. He laid the rifle down and unfolded his glasses from his pocket and put them on. Time was passing, I was getting nervous because the buck was ready to bolt at any second even though he was 350 yards away. Dad put the rifle to his shoulder again and promptly said he still couldn't see the buck. He had always shot a four power scope, but when I had bought the rifle from him, I had replaced the scope with a 3x9 Leupold variable scope which was now set on 4 power. I reached up from where I lay beside him and twisted the scope up to 9 power.

"Now I can see him," he said, and almost simultaneously a shot rang out. The buck hit the ground and didn't move, like as if he had been hit by a low flying jet. I watched the buck with my spotting scope for a couple of minutes and he didn't move. Dad was ready and waiting to shoot again if need be.

At the shot, the surrounding terrain produced a harem of does, which were now hastily making their escape.

I happily shook my dad's hand and congratulated him on the shot. He hadn't lost his shooting touch in the 10 year interval since he had last hunted.

We got his tag out and punched it and I left dad on the rim while I started off down the steep, insecure, rocky slope. We had burned most of our daylight and by the time I arrived at the bottom of the canyon, it was growing blacker by the minute. I went to where I thought the buck should have been, but he wasn't there. Everything looked different, now that I was down in the rocky canyon, than it had looked in better light from a higher angle.

I made a circle around the patch of dark timber and came back through it. I was skirting along the edge of the timber, now totally confused as to the location of the buck. I thought he might have possibly gotten up and run off, but he looked real dead the last time I had seen him. About this time, I walked right into the buck and almost stumbled over him. My instincts had been right or I was just lucky. Either way, I had found the buck. I tagged the big muley and field dressed him by braille. I have field dressed so many head of game in my life in my own hunting and through guiding that it is no problem for me to dress one in the dark if need be.

I scampered back up the incline to where my dad was waiting and told him the buck was a nice, deep forked 6x6 counting brow points and a non-typical point on each side of the back forks. We later scored the buck at 170 Boone & Crockett points.

There was more light on the plateau than in the canyon because the moon was coming up.

We walked straight to the truck and were home in about an hour telling my mother about the hunt and the success. She had kept supper warm for us.

The next day my Dad, myself, and a friend returned to the kill site and photographed the buck, caped it, cut it in half and brought it out of the deep hole. My dad carried out the head and cape which he now has mounted in his living room. My friend and I made two trips to drag out the two halves of meat. Dad helped me get my first big buck and now I helped him get his first and last big buck.

At this writing my father is 75 years old. He still enjoys seeing game and he can still catch more fish than any of the rest of his sons.

Dad said earlier that he "didn't have to shoot a big six pointer", but that is exactly what he got. Thank the Lord.

Even though my dad was a meat hunter, I have always been oriented to trophy hunting. When I was 12 years old, I passed my hunter safety course and bet my instructor that I would shoot a bigger deer than he would. The five point mule deer buck that I shot that fall on October 19, 1958 won me the bet and started me on a career of trophy hunting. This photo was taken on a family antelope hunt near Winnett, Montana in 1955. My dad was 39 years old and I was 9. Davy Crockett was a national hero when I was a boy and this early day hunter had a profound effect on my young mind. I wanted to wear a coonskin cap, hunt bears, be a real woodsman, and wander throughout the wilderness when I grew up.

My dad, Jim Butler, shot this trophy antelope in the 1960's near Winnett, Montana. Dad took several good antelope through the years. Antelope hunting was always a family outing for us. My mother and grandfather also went along. I have many fond memories of these hunting trips. I remember many pleasant hunting experiences with my brothers Jim and Doug also. My father basically quit hunting when he was about the age that I am now, maybe he had endured enough cold camps, steep hills, windy ridge lines and frozen mornings. Maybe he would rather just see an animal instead of shooting it. For whatever reasons a person may stop hunting, they don't have to make excuses to anyone.

As a boy, I was as eager to hunt and kill as a wolf pup. This screech owl was legal game then and I shot it with my Stevens single shot .22 rifle. We all evolve and mature as hunters and humans beings. You couldn't force me to shoot a screech owl now. I recall past hunts with fervor and eagerly anticipate future hunts. When I am in the quiet world of the hunter, I am functioning on a deeper, older, freer plane. I don't kill just to kill anymore. I try to take only the most superb specimens and try to make sure the meat is also used. I do much more hunting and much less killing now, but the predator circuit is incomplete if a hunter doesn't kill occasionally.

October 11, 1959, Montana. This is my first antelope. It is a buck with 1-1/2 inch horns. I stalked it with my lever action Model 94 Winchester, in 30-30 caliber, and killed it in its bed with one shot. I love antelope country, the big, dry, rough, sage covered, lonesome land that allows one to think deeply when he is there. A young person can hone their hunting skills on antelope. Tags are usually easy to draw and you can hunt them almost every year. Some say they don't like antelope meat, but if you kill them quickly and cleanly, before they have been run, and then cool them out thoroughly soon thereafter, antelope can provide some excellent meat and tasty eating.

This is my first black bear, a female that squares about 6 feet. It was big for a female Montana bear. I was hunting with my father near Cooke City and shot the bear through the lungs with my 30-30 Winchester. I was 14 years old at the time, in 1960, and knew nothing about caring for a hide. I nailed it on the back of the garage and scraped off fat and grease for two years. When I failed to get the hide clean enough to take it into my mother's house, we finally took the hide to a taxidermist to be tanned into leather. The hair had long since slipped. Get the hide off a bear as soon as possible and keep it cool and out of the sun until you can get it to a taxidermist. Freeze it if possible.

I have always liked dogs. I literally love hounds. Most of them don't have a mean bone in their body as far as humans are concerned. They are honest, intelligent, loyal, noble, friendly, and adapt to any situation or owner. The saying "true as a hound dogs heart" is well deserved. Hounds also make fine pets as well as hunting dogs. This is my first hound a Redbone-Weimaraner cross. I treed a few coons with him but he wasn't much good for anything except a watchdog. The bearded fellow, Chuck Davis, was a real mountain man who spent months by himself in the wilds. He once caught a 187 lb. mountain lion. I spent a great deal of time with him and learned many secrets of nature from him.

My niece Jody Shields, the daughter of my sister Margie, and I spent a pleasant winter afternoon in the sagebrush draws and juniper covered rocky ridges near my home. We took turns with the 22 rifle and came home with these seven cottontail rabbits. My wife pan fries the rabbit, like chicken, and serves it with mashed potatoes, gravy that is made from the drippings, and all the other fixin's. Yumm! Yumm!

My nephew Jim Shields, the son of my sister Margie, and I with a 5 x 6 whitetail buck that Jim shot with my 30.06. Jim and I sat in a cottonwood tree by a small meadow, the evening of the first day of the season. The buck walked out and stopped at the edge of the meadow, allowing Jim a 125 yard shot. Jim only needed the one shot to collect his first deer. He shot a 4 x 4 whitetail buck on a B tag that year also. In the year that Jim lived with me, he accompanied me on many of my trophy hunts also. Jim's real love is fishing. I remember taking him to catch his first trout, I never saw a kid more excited. Now, Jim fishes as much as he can, preferring it to hunting. Go get em', Jim.

My nephew Jim Shields with his first bull elk taken on the West Rosebud River in Montana. I was looking for a bighorn ram, but spotted this spike bull elk traveling down canyon instead. Jim and I rapidly climbed the mountainside and intercepted the bull at 25 yards as he came out of a patch of quaken aspen. Jim downed the spike with one shot from my 30.06. The young bull provided us with excellent meat that winter. Jim was with me later that fall when I shot a full curl bighorn ram in the same canyon.

My nephew Reese Butler, son of my brother Jim, and I with a large non-typical 7 x 9 point whitetail buck that Reese shot with a 7mm Magnum rifle in mid-November, 1990. Reese had shot mule deer bucks, but now wanted a whitetail, so I asked him to hunt with me one evening. I had been seeing many young whitetail bucks. Reese and I took a ground stand at the edge of a small meadow, with my brother Jim and other nephew Brad, watching another meadow 100 yards away. As Reese and I studied the edge of the brush, some whitetail does came out. Soon a large buck appeared at a primary scrape about 150 yards from us. I whispered to Reese to hold his shot until the buck walked, broadside, out into the meadow towards the does. (Continued on Page 108)...

I would then whistle, stopping the buck for a shot. We were kneeling on the ground and I got buck fever so bad that I had to grab hold of a cottonwood tree to steady myself. I tried to whistle but couldn't. My nephew snickered. I wet my lips, finally whistled, and the buck stopped broadside. Reese took him with one shot in the lungs. The buck scored 170-2/8" non-typical, bigger than any I had ever shot. I think my fear that Reese might miss the big buck caused my worst buck fever in twenty years. GREAT FUN! King of the Mountain camouflage wool clothing blends in great in river bottom whitetail habitat. Above Photo: My younger brother Jim and his son Brad, with Brad's 4 x 4 whitetail taken on Thanksgiving Day after Reese shot his buck on an earlier November hunt. Brad is three years younger than Reese, but has taken four antelope - with the largest one scoring 76 Boone & Crockett points, two mule deer bucks (the largest a 5 x 5), a coyote, a wild turkey, and is working on elk.

Chapter 15

SPRING BLACK BEAR HUNTING

So you want a bear rug huh? Sounds easy enough. Just drive out into the wilds of one of the western states that has a spring black bear season and shoot one. Sometimes it is that easy, but usually not.

There are many ways to hunt black bears in the spring. You can hunt over bait, which is legal in many states. You can run them with hounds, which is also legal in some areas. Or you can go one on one and glass for your bear at long distances and then stalk close enough for a shot. Another way would be to still hunt through a known bear area looking for your trophy bruin.

The first thing to do in your bear quest would be to go to or call the Fish and Game Department in the area you plan to hunt. First you want to know if there is a spring bear season, then whether there are huntable amounts of bears in the area you plan to hunt. Ask to speak to the biologist in the area that is in charge of black bear hunting. Ask him where the best spots are and if he has a map of where kills have been made in the past. Many biologists have this information and will share it with interested hunters.

Ask if grizzly bears are also found in the same area. If the grizzly is also found where you plan to hunt black bears, then you had better have the biologist tell you how to tell the difference in field identification. Many game departments have brochures that show the differences in black bears and grizzlies.

While you are hunting, if you have any question about the identification of a particular bear which you are looking at, then don't shoot! The grizzly is on the threatened species list throughout the continental United States.

Now, getting back to black bears, I did just drive out and shoot one once. I drove a hundred miles from my home one afternoon, up into a beautiful mountain area. I stopped the vehicle, walked to a favorite spot of mine, and started glassing the large partially timbered basin. There were thin stands of quaken aspen, open meadows, and much thicker patches of Douglas fir. I had only glassed about five minutes, when I saw movement below me. I centered the 10 x 25 Zeiss binoculars on the area of the movement and identified a beautiful red-yellow colored bear.

The bear was of the black bear species which can be many different colors from black to chocolate brown to red or blond-yellow or any shade in between. The bear had not seen me and was walking slowly toward me. Bears don't see too well, but they have excellent hearing and sense of smell.

The red and yellow male bear from the high mountains.

The bear was only about 100 yards from me. The wind was still so I knew it would not smell me. I had a camera with a telephoto lens and took three pictures of it as it moseyed up the timber edge toward me. I had never taken a bear of that color before and thought it would make a great rug.

After shooting the bear, I returned home and cared for the meat and the hide. The mounted hide is a beauty to look at and the bear meat tasted best roasted.

A Big Male Black Bear

When I look at the bear rug, I think of that calm, bright spring day in the mountains of Montana.

AUTHOR'S NOTE: I have taken three black bears in Montana in the fall, with this one in the story being the only one taken in the spring. I have taken three black bears in Saskatchewan, Canada, in the spring also. Through both guiding and hunting with friends, I have been in on the kill of quite a few black bears.

I've enjoyed looking at many, many black bears through the years and could have killed most of them but didn't.

The only black bears that have caught my interest for several years are those that score close to the Boone and Crockett Record Book minimum.

Trophy hunting is better conservation. If you don't see the old bruiser you want, then don't shoot. It won't make you any less of a person to not fill a tag, it may make you a better person for not having shot.

Chocolate colored, male Black Bear with a white "v" on his chest, squaring 6 foot, taken in east central Saskatchewan, Canada. I was hunting in the spring season, by myself, before Saskatchewan required that you hunt with a guide. I was hunting over bait in a remote area, near the Manitoba border, that was forty miles across between roads. It was drizzling rain as I sat about 50 yards from the bait on an evening hunt. The bear appeared from my left front, walking towards the bait. He heard me start to remove my scope cover, and stopped. He sniffed the air, but the wind was in my favor. When he resumed walking, I took him with a lung shot.

I took this 500 lb. male black bear on May 21 in east central Saskatchewan. He was number 15 in Safari Club International Record Book when I got him. He made the Boone & Crockett awards book also with a score of 20-6/16 points. Self-guided.

Chapter 16

MOUNTAIN GOAT - DANGEROUS HUNTING

Nothing usually goes wrong on a hunt. I have hunted many thousands of days in my forty years of hunting, having started with a BB gun when I was 6 years old. Normally, you go out to hunt and sometimes small unpredictable things happen that are not life threatening, but make a hunt memorable. Things like seeing an animal do something that you have never seen one do before or some particularly spectacular scenery or view that is seen in a different way only on that one day because of special lighting, time of day, or season combination, that will stick in your mind for as long as you have memory.

But sometimes, one small misstep, one bad judgement, out of thousands of good decisions, because of fatigue, hurry, taking a chance, or one bad piece of luck, can kill you or somewhat threaten your life, so that the experience is always crystal clear in your mind forever after, reminding you never to make that mistake again.

October 21:

I left my home in south central Montana, near Billings and drove the long 375 miles westward to Hamilton in the Bitterroot Valley of Montana, arriving in late evening.

I would stay the night with my friend, Leland Crow, who was in his early 80's and had lived the life of a hunter. Leland had taken most of the common western animals, and on a walking postman's salary, had taken a grand slam of wild sheep, polar bear and other exotic animals. I was particularly impressed with a big typical mule deer, scoring about 195 Boone & Crockett points, he had taken in Idaho when he was 80 years old. Some people are born to hunt and are driven by an unseen instinct, to pursue game all their lives. Leland is now 90 years old, but as recently as two years ago, he shot a muskox in the arctic of northern Canada.

The next morning, after an enjoyable evening of campfire talk, even though we sat in Leland's living room, I arranged my pack and got ready to go to the nearby mountains.

I had drawn a mountain goat tag for the Bitterroot Mountain Range and would backpack in to hunt on my own for several days.

It was now the twenty-first of October, and I had waited this far into the season so that the goats would have better hair. The long hair on a goat is half the trophy anyway. If you wait too late in the season to hunt, however, the deep snows restrict your travel, and you might have to shoot a smaller goat, because you may not have as many goats to choose from.

I checked with a couple of game wardens and they said that only about six goats had been taken so far, none over six inches in length.

The year before, a friend of mine had taken an 8-1/2 inch billy up Roaring Lion Creek. He said he had seen nine billy goats in both the head of Roaring Lion and Sawtooth Creeks.

Leland Crow dropped me off at the trail head, up Roaring Lion Creek at 1:30 p.m.

At about four miles in, I saw a seven inch billy by himself. That was the only goat I saw on that first day of hunting, even though I glassed a lot.

The woods smelled like musty wet wood, pungent frost crisped ferns and mushrooms, and the ever present pine aroma, that you smell on a fresh black bear hide, or mountain sheep, deer, or elks horns when they are fresh and have lived their lives in the mountains.

I hiked and hunted until 6:30 p.m. and stopped at the Dust Camp for the night. It was a nice camp site, flat and dry, by the creek. I ate supper of oatmeal, eggnog and a small candy bar. I didn't eat much that day. I took a vitamin pill and downed some salt tablets, so I wouldn't have muscle cramps after my first day of exertion on the trail. The sky was fairly clear and I went to bed at 8:30 p.m. to let the rushing creek sing me to sleep.

I lay awake for awhile thinking about the coyote tracks, goat tracks and black bear sign I had seen on the trail on the way in earlier that day. I had seen no deer or elk sign, though. It would be a long night, with many hours until daylight.

October 22:

The sky was cloudy this morning. As I broke camp, I noticed one of my fiberglass tent poles had a split in the end of it. I tried to repair it and hoped it would last out the hunt.

On the north side of the trail, I saw a nannie goat with a fuzzy kid, and a little further on, another nannie and kid. I located a nice cream colored billy goat with nine inch horns, but decided to pass him up because it was fairly early in the season.

The cloud cover kept getting heavier as the day progressed and it started to rain about 3:30 p.m. I got under a big, umbrella shaped, spruce tree and waited for the rain to stop. Looking upward in the steep sided canyon, I could see the heavy clouds drifting and shifting and the rain came in intermittent sheets. A typical mountain storm. I love them.

About 4:30 p.m. I whipped up some chicken stew and added diced

beef for protein. This stew, two candy bars, and a couple of cups of cold water made up my meal. The rain showed no signs of quitting by dark, so I pitched camp in this relatively dry place, under the broad spruce by the edge of the trail.

I had seen elk, mule deer, and mountain goat tracks in the trail this day.

It was still raining at 7:30 p.m. when I went to bed. Real quiet here. Not any kind of civilized noise, just the rain and wind in the evergreens. I will hunt tomorrow, rain or shine.

October 23:

I arose early and it was snowing in light squalls. It is easy to get up on mornings after 12 hours in the sleeping bag.

It was starting to clear and the sky would be mostly clear by evening. I hunted hard, covering a lot of country and glassed 12 goats with the largest, having only an eight inch horn.

Eight men with 16 horses and pack mules came in and set up their camp above me on the creek.

I dined on beef stew that evening.

Stars shining, creek roaring, Bill sleeping.

October 24:

I was up before daylight in the snapping cold morning, and soon after dawn, saw three goats.

I climbed for a better part of the day, and once on top, looked into the Sawtooth drainage to the north. I didn't see any goats in the new canyon and also glassed back into Roaring Lion Creek from this elevated position. I didn't see any more goats besides the ones I had seen early that morning. Much more quickly than I had ascended the mountain, I descended it.

After my turkey noodle soup meal, I rehydrated with four cups of dehydrated milk, mixed in water.

I spent two hours with the hunters that were camped about a quarter of a mile above me. They were looking for some winter meat and a pleasant outing.

It was clear again that night, as it had been all day.

Tomorrow would be the first day of the deer and elk season and I would have to leave the goat country for now. I would come back in November and hoped to find a better goat area, with more mature billies to choose from.

Once back home, one thing led to another and I was unable to return until the 25th of November. I would be able only to hunt on the 26th, with the season closing on the 27th.

A friend's two fourteen year old sons were to hunt with me that day.

118

They would hunt mule deer and elk near the bottom of the canyon while I would climb high for goat.

I hiked up Fred Burr Canyon about five miles to a small lake. The boys would hunt their way in looking for deer and elk on the canyon sides. We were to meet at the little man-made reservoir in late afternoon.

As soon as I arrived at the lake, I spotted some goats high up in some rocks on the north face of the canyon wall.

The air currents were drifting down the canyon. I planned to climb the steep mountain on the downwind side, until I was slightly above the goats' position, and then sneak out along a ledge above a cliffy area, until I could get a clear shot, if there was a big billy goat present to shoot.

The snow was about 18 inches deep, and the climbing was slow and tedious. It took me most of the day to gain enough elevation to put my plan into effect.

Once I thought I was higher than the goats, I started sneaking around the mountain. The way was treacherous, with a dropoff on my left. The foot and a half of wet snow actually gave me a more secure footing.

I was wearing a white suit with my hunter orange vest over it. I figured that if animals are color blind, then an orange vest blends fairly well with a white suit.

I peeked over a small rock shelf right into the eyes of a big nannie goat at about 30 yards. The wind was still in my face, so she could not smell me, but she thought I looked out of place. She stood staring at me a short time, probably thinking I was another goat, then she started to climb above me.

After the nannie gained more altitude than me, she came around above me and was coming down behind me to get my scent.

About this time, a lone billy that had been out of sight on the small incline between cliffs, stepped out where I could see him. I had nothing by which to judge his size, no other goats for body comparison, only the length of his horn in relationship to the distance between his eye and his nostril. It was late afternoon of my last day to hunt, and although I wasn't certain of his size, he was mature and probably my last chance to fill my rarely drawn goat tag.

The nannie goat was now almost down to my level and would soon smell me and spook, also spooking the billy.

The shot was short, about 50 yards, and I took it quickly from a sitting position. The billy went down in the deep snow and didn't move.

I looked and the nanny's tracks were right behind me. I saw her above me now, hurriedly making tracks for higher ground. I painstakingly climbed down the near vertical face, to the prostrate male goat. The light was fading fast, as I tagged the goat, took a photo, skinned him, and

The mountain goat from the dangerous cliffs.

boned all the meat, which I put into my backpack. I tied the skin and head on the top of the pack.

Not wanting to climb back through the cliffs the way I had come earlier in the day in good light, I now looked below me for a way down. Off to my right, I saw a snow chute running down between the cliffs to an area where I could reach the scattered timber near the bottom and have good going clear to the trail.

I would have to get down the snow chute first. I had gone down many of these before and didn't think this one would be a problem. I looked about half way down the narrow channel and saw a large bush growing along its edge. I thought if I did slip, and start to slide, that I could grab this bush when I got to it and stop myself.

I started inching my way down the slide, my body sideways, with my right shoulder next to the mountain. This way, my snow packs would be horizontal to the face, and would benefit from the bite of the whole track on the snow instead of just the heel as if I walked straight down. Things were going fine for a short distance, then my feet gave way from under me and I was streaking down the passageway, picking up speed as I went. I saw the bush coming and grabbed at it with my right hand, my arm immediately being jerked up and back, dislocating it at the shoulder. The arm trailed uselessly behind me now, and there was excruciating pain as I continued downward. My mind raced futily for a plan, but there was none. My weight, combined with the weight of my full pack, pushed me ever faster.

In about the length of time that it takes to rear end someone on an icy road, I rocketed down the chute, off a small cliff, and landed head first into a deep snow pile at the bottom, with the heavy pack lurching forward to pin me face down in the snow. The snow was about three feet deep, and it cushioned my landing.

I was chambered like a shotgun shell, head first down between two big boulders. My first thought was, could I move or had I broken my neck or back and become paralyzed. I kicked my legs and they worked. I moved my neck and head from side to side trying to make room enough to breath in the damp snow. My left arm was under my chest and my right arm was twisted around behind my back, still of no use.

You might think that a person would be frightened at a time like this. As I came down the chute, my only thoughts were how to stop myself. There was not time to fear.

Now at the bottom, ignominiously stuck head down, feet up, between two rocks in deep snow, my only emotion was rage. I knew in my heart that I was not going to stay there and suffocate or freeze to death.

Have you ever done a lot of pushups and then when thoroughly tired, tried to do one more? That last push up is what it was like to push myself, my rifle, and the heavy pack, up and out of the hole. I squirmed with my legs also, and tried to gain leverage to keep me from slipping back. All this time I was still in a fighting mad rage. My adrenalin fueled me. I pushed steadily upward and wouldn't allow myself to weaken and slip back.

Then I cleared the top of a rock and was able to roll onto my back. I struggled out of the pack and got to my feet, madder than a buzzed up hornet. Luckily, I was able to quickly get my shoulder back in the socket.

I looked at my rifle and it was banged up a bit but I hadn't broken the stock. I glanced at the goat horns and they were not broken either.

With my left arm, I negotiated the pack full of meat to the top of a rock and painfully struggled back into the harness, picked up my rifle and started down the slope, now not so steep, toward the main trail.

It was dark when I reached the lake where the boys were waiting. I told them what had happened, and they offered to carry my pack and the rifle. I handed the rifle to one of them, but kept the pack as it would have been too heavy for them to pack for the five miles we had to go down the trail to the vehicle, and too painful to keep changing back and forth.

The boys weren't successful on their deer and elk hunt that day.

One of the lads got a Mini Maglite out of my pack and we trudged down the winding snow covered path, arriving at the pickup some time later.

The 8-3/4 inch mountain goat trophy was hard won.

If you want to hunt goats, do it earlier in the season, allowing enough time to find a big one. Don't hunt after the snow gets deep and perilous.

Other people look at the trophies on my wall and say "that one is nice" and look on to the next one, without realizing just how difficult or dangerous it was to collect some of these animals.

HUNTING TIPS:

When you are in sheep and goat country and climbing, there is usually a fairly level shelf along the base of a cliff that you can easily walk.

When climbing down a steep hillside, stay in the timber if the snow is not too deep there so you can grab hold of the trees to stop you from sliding.

If you are in deep snow on a steep hillside, stay next to the timber if possible in case of an avalanche so you can move into the trees out of the path of the sliding snow.

When climbing in a chute, be extremely careful of dry leaves, wet moss, or loose rocks and gravel. They are very slick and could cause a bad fall.

If you fall on a steep hillside and start sliding, try to turn onto your stomach and dig into the side hill with feet and hands to stop your slide.

Mountain Goat taken in the Rock Creek Drainage in the Beartooth Mountains of Montana. The billy had 9 inch long horns with 5-1/2 inch bases. I shot him on a one day hunt on the last day of the season, November 23rd, allowing for optimum hair growth for my trophy mount. I have only drawn two goat tags in Montana, with this one being the first. Hunting on snow while wearing white camouflage makes you almost invisible to most game animal's sharp eyes. I believe mountain goats think you are another goat, when you are dressed in white. Once my brother Jim, and I, were hunting on green grass in the early season before the first snowfall. Jim's goat hunt was a two-day affair. We backpacked into the Beartooth Mountains ten miles on Saturday and camped over night. On Sunday, we spotted three billy goats. We wore white camouflage and stalked the billy goats while remaining in plain sight of them. We were able to walk up to within 175 yards of the goats, choose the goat we wanted, and Jim shot it. If you draw a mountain goat tag, I recommend that you hunt from about October 15 onward, because the goats will have sufficient hair after this date to be a beautiful trophy. You should hunt before the mountains are covered with heavy snowfall, because you can traverse more country without being hampered by the snow. Sometimes you have to cover a lot of country to find a trophy mountain goat.

Montana Pronghorn Antelope

People say "what does it matter what I do now, no one will care a hundred years from now anyway." Don't be fooled, what you do now determines what your soul will be doing in a hundred years from now.

Bill Butler-December 30, 1992

Chapter 17
PASS SHOOTING ANTELOPE

The eastern sky was rapidly turning yellow as I stepped from the warmth of my Ford Bronco. Frosted grass crunched under foot as I removed the 30.06 from its case, jammed a few shells in it, put some more into my pocket, and started walking up an open ridge. The early morning October cold bit at my nose and ears as I walked in a gently rushing crosswind.

My brother, Doug, and I had camped the night before, next to a haystack in an alfalfa field. We were on a friend's ranch near Winnett, Montana. We had hunted this area many times before and knew it well.

I had dropped Doug off already to go to his prechosen spot. We had not seen any hunters the day before when we had glassed some of the herds, but now I could see some headlights moving up the winding dirt roads. Usually I don't care to hunt where many other hunters hunt, but with antelope, sometimes you can benefit from the presence of other hunters.

I finally arrived at a high pass through the ridge just as the top edge of the sun appeared on the horizon. I picked a spot where I could see well down into the pass, and also could view the expanses that stretched away from each side of the ridge.

I lay down on my stomach in the tall sagebrush with my rifle and spotting scope and waited. I had heard a few shots already but now as the sun cleared the skyline and lit the countryside, I started to hear shots from locations all over the prairie. I could see hunters, hear the sounds of the shots, and see antelope now running in large bunches.

As I watched through my spotting scope some hunters killed antelope. The antelope split up into smaller bunches. Many had come through the pass, mostly does and fawns with some small immature bucks. One bunch came up the ridge behind me and veered off only when I sat up in front of them.

I had seen a few nice bucks go by out of range. I waited. The sun got hotter. Then about 11:00 a.m. I spotted a lone buck at about one mile, coming my way. He was loping in the typical hobby-horse antelope gait. He came straight on towards the gap to within a half mile but was veered off by other hunters. I watched him through the scope. He carried long, heavy black horns that stood up fairly close together.

When he was out of range of the other hunters, the buck changed direction again and came straight through the pass. When the buck was about 125 yards away I shot. He never knew what hit him.

If you want a big buck antelope this fall on the first day of the season when other hunters are moving the antelope around, take advantage of the antelope's tendency to travel through passes and you will score.

This is the antelope buck that I shot while pass shooting.

In the late 1970's, my friend Terry Bateman told me, "If mice had horns they'd never get you out of the barn."

My nephew, Jim Shields, was with me when I got this 15 inch antelope northeast of Jordan, Montana in Garfield County. I had shot a 17 inch (green) buck the year before that made Boone & Crockett (82-2/8) and also Safari Club International Record Book. To show you how badly you can misjudge trophy antelope, I thought this buck would make B&C when I shot it. The buck was laying alone, away from his does. After I made a stalk to within 100 yards of the buck using a small butte for cover, I easily collected him. He had a very small body and in proportion his horns looked huge but only scored 75-4/8. Compare a buck's body size to other bucks or even does before you shoot. Wait them out if you have to.

Jim's Missouri Breaks 7 x 7 trophy bull elk.

Your total life on earth is just an entrance exam for the life hereafter.
Bill Butler 7-30-1990

Chapter 18

MAJESTIC BULL ELK
IN THE MISSOURI BREAKS

Most hunters that come out west to hunt would rather have a big bull elk than any other trophy.

I have guided hunters to several big bulls through the years, but the largest that I have ever taken myself is a 5x5.

On a bitter cold morning once, I had two of my hunters take two big 6x6 bulls close together on a snow covered alpine ridge.

I don't know why, but so far elk haven't turned me on very much. When I was guiding, I didn't usually have very much time to hunt on my own, for myself. In order to have winter meat, I would shoot the first legal bull that I saw. Most of the bull elk I have shot have been spikes for the freezer. Elk are about the only Montana big game animal that I haven't trophy hunted much. My priority has always been to hunt the other species of the state.

When I was busy trying to take the Montana Big Ten, if I had any spare time, I would hunt a species that I hadn't taken before.

Because I have guided for several big bull elk, and have seen quite a number of other immense racks that other hunters have taken, notably in the Gardiner, Montana area, an elk rack has to score over 330 Boone & Crockett points before I'm very impressed.

Maybe I guided too much for elk and got burned out on hunting them. I do this on different species because I hunt them so intensely and when I do burn out on a particular species, then I don't hunt them much for awhile.

As I write this, December 1992, I feel that I am ready to seriously hunt elk and put a big bull or two on my wall. I plan to start bowhunting for them because the bowhunting season will give me access to giant bulls during the rut and also access to hunting areas where I have been unable to draw a gun tag. Even though I might be using a bow, I am not going to lower my standards to just kill a bull elk. I have well defined parameters of what I think a trophy bull is and will not lower them, just to say I got one with a bow.

As I have said, I haven't been the one to pull the trigger on an enormous bull elk, but I have been a party to the taking of some pretty good ones. The following is the story of the best bull elk that I have had the privilege of helping bring to bag.

I had guided bow hunters to several elk in the Missouri Breaks in the early 1980's. Hunters missed the two very best bulls that we saw, 330 and a 360 pointers. I saw a lot of real big bulls and, with much anticipation, started putting in for a gun tag.

To my way of thinking, bowhunting takes a lot of time, and I wasn't ready to make a commitment to that kind of time expenditure in that period of my life. I have yet to draw a gun tag for elk in 12 years of applying in the Missouri Breaks.

I suggested to my brother, Jim, that he should put in also. Jim had killed some elk with his bow in the Breaks, but like me, was unable to devote the time to hunt a big bull successfully. Jim drew a gun tag on his first try.

The season would open on the 17th of October and we arrived on the 16th. We already knew the lay of the country and where we had seen big bulls before. We set up our camp in a grove of stately cottonwoods next to the meandering Missouri River. After a hot meal we got a good night's sleep.

The next morning, by the time the sky started to lighten, we were ready and waiting to start glassing from a prominent hilltop overlooking the wide river valley. We searched the river bottoms thoroughly with spotting scope and binoculars. We scrutinized each red willow patch, cottonwood grove, dry meadow, and brush edge.

Then I saw him. As soon as I saw the old bull I knew he was big. He had super long royal points and the fifth point following on each side was almost equally as long. I could see he had a seventh point on each side also. Jim and I had only a fleeting look at the bull before him and his eight cows drifted into some willows to bed for the day.

Jim and I had a war council on how to get the old veteran. Jim was inclined to sneak in after the bull in the willows, which he had done successfully with his bow, on previous trips.

The elk were on a point of land in the bend of the river and we watched them long enough to know that they weren't going to leave, but had bedded down for the day.

We hadn't seen any other hunters and I didn't think that the elk would be disturbed throughout the day if we left them alone. It was hard to talk Jim into waiting until afternoon, but I convinced him that he should not take the unnecessary risk of possibly spooking the elk out of their beds and maybe not get a shot.

It has been my experience that if elk are not disturbed, they will come back out in the evening, fairly close to where you last saw them disappear into the cover that morning.

We went to camp and spent an anxious day waiting. About 4:00 p.m. we returned to the area of the elk and Jim went into the location on foot. I stayed up on the ridge and watched the unfolding drama with my spotting scope. Two people just complicate a hunt and although I would like to have been with him, I knew he would have a better chance at the big elk alone.

I watched Jim as he selected a ground stand, downwind from where the elk had faded into the willows that morning. We waited until the diminishing sun went down but the elk didn't show up exactly where they had gone in the cover that morning.

There was a half an hour of legal shooting time left.

Jim heard some crashing around through the brush and willows off to his right. He started to crawl on his hands and knees through some short willows, over towards the area of the noise. Then he stopped abruptly. There was a cow elk and the big 7 point bull, out there ahead of him in a clearing. Jim got a solid rest over a log with his 7mm rifle and located the buckskin bull in the scope. The cow was standing in front of the bull and Jim figured he'd better shoot right away as soon as the cow moved because the bull was standing between two trees and in about two steps would be behind one of the trees.

The light was deteriorating fast but there was still plenty enough remaining for a good shot. As soon as the cow moved, the bull turned broadside and Jim shot it through the lungs. Jim immediately put another round in the chamber and looked at the bull through his scope. The bull never moved but just stood there. The cow hadn't run either. They didn't know what had happened. Then the bull went down and laid still. Good lung shots don't take long to work.

Jim stood up and took a couple of steps toward the elk and then the skittish cow spooked, and ran about 20 yards to his right, stopped, turned around and then ran on into the darkening willows.

Jim signaled me to come down. I had seen the cow after the shot but had never seen the bull. I rushed down the hill and soon joined Jim in the opening.

The bull was beautiful with his tan body, and reddish cape and head. He had 14 long, chocolate colored tines, with ivory white tips. Handshakes and congratulations. We tagged, photographed and gutted the elk and then pulled the bull up off the ground on some small cottonwood logs so that the brisk night air would cool the underside of the bull. It had been fairly chilly at night and we weren't worried about the meat spoiling. We propped it open to help cool the meat also.

The next day we came back and after taking more photos in the better light, we caped and quartered the elk.

Jim's back was bothering him from an old injury, so I packed each of the four quarters out on my back. By the way I had to go, it was about a mile one way to the truck.

Jim has a shoulder mount in his home of the fine bull, which scores 352 Boone & Crockett points net.

I didn't shoot this elk. I guided a hunter in his seventies to this fine bull near Gardiner, Montana on a November hunt. It was the last week of the season and we had good snow cover. I had two hunters positioned about two hundred yards apart, myself and one on the crest of the ridge and the other fellow was watching an open area down the ridge below us. As the other guides made a push up the ridge, the two six pointers came out ahead of them. We were in the right place at the right time and got both bulls. We took six big bulls that week with me guiding for three of them.

Chapter 19

SHED ANTLER HUNTING

I left the house about an hour before dark and diagonaled across the corn field toward the river. It was spring time in the Clark's Fork Valley. The sun was low in the west and glowed its warmth deep into my skin. As I strode on the tops of the corn furrows with some of the yet standing, stripped stalks rubbing against my denim pants and nylon down coat, I heard a rush of wings as some mallards came in to feed. Whitetail deer tracks were everywhere in the slightly moist, rich brown earth. I was going to the woods below, that bordered the river, to look for shed antlers of the large whitetail buck that lived in a few square miles near my home.

I reached a fence at the edge of the timber, stepped over it, and headed towards the thickest part of the stovepipe sized cottonwoods. The buck bedded here often, and may have caught his horn on a bush nearby and pulled it off when it became loose enough to fall.

I moved slowly through the timber. The old brown leaves, disintegrating and dirty, lay where they had been flattened by the snows of the winter. I kept looking all around for the shed antlers and also for the live deer as they would slip out ahead of me. I saw the flag of one that did, as he loped in his rocking horse gait across an opening ahead of me.

I was now to the edge of the river, standing in some red willows. I could see some backwater of the river directly in front of me and there were four greenheaded mallards swimming on it. One of the drakes had seen me and was getting nervous. I stepped out of the willows, on to the bank and the mallards jumped into the air and rapidly climbed away.

I walked on in the darkening evening and saw a great blue heron rise off a gravel bar and flap slowly away to find a more lonely fishing hole. A drake and hen merganser beat down the river, running on the water at first, then becoming airborne. I turned, once again, into the woods to look for the shed antlers. Soon I noticed five ivory points and knew that I had found my trophy.

Whitetail bucks lose their antlers any where from late December until sometime in March with the older bucks losing theirs first. I like to find the horns of the big bucks especially, to know if they made it through the past hunting season.

By picking up the antlers, a person can tell exactly how big the deer are in an area and can then concentrate his fall hunting on a region where he has found the largest set of antlers the spring before.

I find most of my antlers on trails in brush areas where the deer have

Non-typical Mule Deer Buck

bumped something, such as a branch or tree, to dislodge the loose antler when the time comes for shedding. Occasionally, I do find them in open fields and even on roadsides where the deer have jarred the antlers loose when jumping a fence. Many can also be found in thick brush where the deer bed down. I have even stepped on them after they have been covered with leaves. If they are upside down, your foot will usually slip off, exposing them, or if they are right side up, they will rock since they are basket shaped.

Deer, elk, and moose all shed their antlers on their winter range. So, when you find an area where these game animals have spent the winter, you will usually find many antlers around in a relatively small area.

134

Chapter 20

MONTANA BIGHORN SHEEP HUNTING

The December day was clear and cold and bright. The kind where everything remains frozen and crackling all day. The big ram had just walked out into an opening between fingers of timber that ran down towards the bottom of the canyon from a solid mass of timber above. A mile above this was an open plateau of the Beartooth Mountains. The ram had just come from the back country to this winter area for the beginning of the annual rut.

My brother, Doug and I watched the ram with spotting scopes on 60 power as I planned my stalk. The ram was a half a mile away and not alerted to our presence. I would follow behind a finger of timber on the steep mountainside until I got close enough for a shot. Doug would give me hand signals as to where the ram was and if I had spooked it or not. I started up the steep mountainside and the going was not good, with a foot of new snow covering everything, including large boulders and holes. I climbed steadily in the brisk evening air and stopped occasionally for Doug's hand signal that said that the ram was still above and to my left. I could not see the ram yet, because of the timber and a rise of ground between him and I. I planned to climb parallel to the ram and then sneak through the timber for a close shot. I had never taken a ram before, and did not want to lose this one, as I had been looking for three years now without success.

When I figured I was within 200 yards of the ram I stopped and looked at Doug. His arm-waving a half mile away indicated that the ram was spooked and running. I turned and ran through the trees to my left and burst into the opening to see the ram standing broadside, looking back up the hill where he had just come from. There was no wind and the ram had not seen me. He had run about 50 yards down the hill and did not appear spooked. I later learned that sheep do this often for no apparent reason.

He now started looking around slowly, but not as if he were looking for anything in particular. From where I was standing it was about 200 yards to the ram. There was a small rise of ground between him and I and if I laid down or even knelt for a steadier shot I could not see the ram. I was blowing from the run at high altitude and did not want to chance an offhand shot.

Since the ram had not seen me, I thought I would sneak from tree to tree in the scattered, pine timber of the edge of the finger until I was above the rise. Then I would have a good rested shot. I started from one tree to the next while the ram was looking away. He had been turning

My first Bighorn Ram, a 7/8 curl.

his head slowly and I thought I had enough time to cover the distance between the trees before he looked back. I looked at the boulder-strewn ground as I moved so as not to trip and fall. At about half way between trees, I looked at the ram to check whether he was still looking up the hill. He was not. His eyes were fixed squarely upon me. I looked at him through my rifle scope on 9 power and he did not look alarmed. His eyes were not wide, his nostrils not flared, and he did not appear nervous.

As I said, I did not want to shoot offhand. I thought the only thing to do was to push my luck and walk straight towards him for 25 yards until I came to the crest of the small rise of ground and I could lay down and shoot. This I did, with him not moving a muscle, until the 30-06, 180 grain bullet hit him in the rib cage. He took two steps forward and then nose-dived and slid 20 yards toward me on the steep hill. I had a fine, dark-bodied ram with over 15 inch bases and 33-1/2 inch curl.

I killed that ram on December 5, 1968, it was my first bighorn sheep.

My brother, Doug, has taken two bighorn rams. His first one was taken the same day as my first one in 1968 only in a different drainage twenty miles away. I was in on both hunts and followed every move with my spotting scope. The stalks were very similar, both from below, and neither ram knew Doug was around until they were hit. They both had ewes, lambs and young rams with them, and these moved off a short distance and began to feed again after the shooting of the ram. These sheep were up and feeding at the time in scattered timber and open meadows on a mountainside. Doug had plenty of available cover and the wind was right for a stalk. There was no need for a stalk from above, as is almost always recommended in every sheep hunting story I read. These rams were 3/4 and 4/5 curl.

I got a chance at a second bighorn in 1969, a full curl. He was with a 4/5 curl ram on a mountainside similar to where I got my first one. I stalked to within 300 yards from below, and was not able to get any closer because there was no more cover. I rested the 30-06 over a large rock, with my down cap underneath, and centered the crosshairs on the top of the back of the larger ram as they lay looking out over the valley. At the shot, both rams were up and running and I expected the big ram to fall at any second, because I had several one-shot kills previous to that already that fall.

The ram didn't fall, but ran into the trees with the younger 4/5 curl ram. Had the great rifleman missed? Had Casey missed the third strike? You bet. My smugness wore thin as I dejectedly walked up to check the shot. I still thought the ram may have been hit somewhere. He wasn't unless you want to count cutting hair from the top of his back just behind the shoulder. I tracked them to the edge of the timber and there was no blood. It was still early, about noon, so I decided to track the rams. I had successfully tracked up other game and killed it, but was skeptical about tracking sheep, as I had heard they completely leave the country once shot at. I tracked the rams for several hours through dog hair pine so thick that I spent much of the time on my hands and knees. Some of the places were so tight that I didn't see how a bighorn sheep could get through and under it.

Bighorns spend a lot of time in the timber and at timber line, as evidenced by the pitch around the base of their horns. They rub their horns against trees much the way deer and elk do, not to shed velvet which they don't have, but to get rid of ticks around the base of the horns by building up pitch in the hair.

I tracked the sheep until late afternoon and was ready to turn back when I looked way up the mountain towards timber line and saw what I thought was a ram. I put the scope on it and sure enough it was the full curl standing looking at me. The other ram was laying down. I was determined not to make any mistakes this time. I crossed over to the far

My second Bighorn Ram, a full curl.

side of the ridge the rams were on, and taking bearings on a castle rock near them, started another stalk.

Later, as I crawled back over the ridge concealed by the lower branches of a big fir tree, I could see the rams about 75 yards from me, with the 4/5 curl still laying down. As I got into shooting position, prone with the gun barrel rested over a large branch, the 4/5 curl ram jumped to his feet and both stood ready for flight as the -06 roared again. This time the larger ram fell sideways over a 10 foot cliff and lay still. As I walked up to the ram, I marvelled at his beauty and thought of the delicious meat I would eat all winter.

A blizzard was just starting, so I tagged the ram, field dressed it, and then caped it. I would come back in a few days after the blizzard quit and get the meat, bone it and carry it out in a backpack.

I saw the other smaller ram several times during the next week as I was deer hunting. I could have gotten a guided hunter a shot at him if I would have had one booked at the time.

Chapter 21

HOW TO HUNT BIGHORN SHEEP IN MONTANA'S AREA 501

I guided hunters for Bighorn Sheep in this area for several years, taking many rams. I have personally shot five rams in the Beartooth Mountains, more than any other hunter.

When I decided to quit guiding for Bighorn Sheep, I revealed all my secrets for hunting this area to Jack Atcheson, Jr. of Butte, Montana, who had been operating in Area 502 previously. He has become quite successful hunting bighorns in Area 501 since then. He is the only licensed guide to hunt sheep in this area now. If you don't want to try to hunt this area on your own, call Jack, Jr., and he may be able to guide you. His phone number is (406) 782-3498.

PART I - LOGISTICS

1.   Area:
Beartooth Mountains. South Central Montana. Bighorn Sheep hunting Area 501.
2.   Nearest Large Town:
Billings, Montana. Population 100,000.
3.   Nearest Small Town:
Absarokee, Montana; Fishtail, Montana; Nye, Montana; Roscoe, Montana.
4.   Description of Area:
This area is made up of high, very rugged plateaus and peaks. Some of which are over 12,000 feet high. There are many cirques, headwalls, peaks, talus slopes, plateaus and streams. It is true high alpine country. There is a good grass cover on the plateaus with much exposed rock. There are a variety of trees including Lodgepole Pine, Douglas Fir, Quaken Aspen lower down and in the low valleys, some willow. The scenery can rival any in North America. You can see a long way and can glass many square miles from one point.
5.   Weather to Expect on September 10:
Seasonal norms National Weather Service - temperature high 74 degrees, low 48 degrees. Daily average 61 degrees. Precipitation .04 inches per day, September monthly 1.26 inches. The weather here in September can vary from 70 degrees above to zero; you can have an autumnal equinox storm in September as the seasons change. It can be

quite severe, but usually lasts only 1 to 3 days with Indian summer following for 2 or 3 weeks. Do not depend on this Indian summer though. If it starts to snow heavily, pull camp and drop elevation as fast as possible to the canyon bottom. Here you can wait to see what the storm will do. If it stays bad, come out of the mountains. If it quits, go back up and hunt. These early storms usually are over quick and melt off in a couple of days, but don't depend on that happening. Some years winter comes early and stays.

6.   Game Counts:

The Bighorn Sheep are widely scattered in this area. They are extremely unpredictable and you may see one anywhere. There is a huntable herd of rams in the Beartooths. I see several legal rams on the winter range every year while photographing after hunting season closes. Some of the older rams don't come to the winter range, but winter high up on wind blown plateaus.

7.   Trophy Probability:

Legal Bighorn Rams run from 27" to 40". There are some rams listed in Boone and Crockett and Safari Club International Record Books that have come from the Beartooths.

8.   Hunting Pressure:

Hunting pressure is heaviest at the first part of the season. After the first snow or two, most everybody leaves. After this it is more dangerous to hunt because of getting caught in a blizzard and snowed in. The hunting is better then because sheep will be forced out of the timber where the snow is deep. Many more sheep also show up from the summer range in Yellowstone Park and other sheep summering areas.

9.   Hospitals:

Billings-Deaconess Medical Center   St. Vincent Hospital
Broadway at 9th Ave N   1233 N. 30th Street
(406) 657-4000   (406) 657-7000
                                     Help Helicopter
                                     1-800-538-4357

10.   Meat Processing Plants:

Billings - 4th Avenue Meat Market & Lockers 252-5686
1718 4th Avenue North

Meat and Poultry Palace - 252-9515
821 16th West

11.   Water Availability:

Drinking water can be obtained from streams in area. Smaller streams toward their source are less contaminated by animals. For your

I shot this Bighorn ram on October 8, near Cooke City, Montana. He was a full curl in his eighth fall of life. I had spotted this ram and another on Index Peak in Wyoming. They were in their summering area and were near the Montana state line. I watched them for two weeks until a snow storm forced them down the mountain and across the state line into Montana. Early the next day, a friend and I climbed the mountain and found the full curl rams bedded in a small pocket for protection from the storm. We connected with good shots and then the work began. We had to carry the head and capes and boned meat down the mountain and to the vehicle. My number three bighorn out of the Beartooth Mountains.

own peace of mind, you should bring water purification equipment. I have had giardia and it is no fun.

12. Airport:
    Billings - Billings Logan International Airport.
    Laurel - small airport.
    Columbus - small airport.
13. Vehicle Rental:
    Avis, Thrifty, Budget, Triple A, Ace, Rent-A-Wreck, Hertz, National, and Dollar, in Billings.
14. Motels:
    Billings, Columbus, Absarokee, Laurel, Fishtail.
15. Gas Stations:
    Billings, Laurel, Columbus, Absarokee, Fishtail, Montana.
16. Cafes:
    Billings, Laurel, Columbus, Absarokee, Fishtail, and sandwiches in Nye, Montana.
17. Grocery Stores:
    Billings, Laurel, Columbus, Absarokee, Fishtail, Montana.
18. Post Offices:
    Billings, Laurel, Columbus, Absarokee, Fishtail, Montana.
19. Churches:
    Billings, Laurel, Columbus, Absarokee, Fishtail, Montana.
20. Sporting Good Stores:

Scheels Sport Shops	Big Bear Sports
1233 24th Street West	Rimrock Mall-24th St. W.
Billings, 656-9220	Billings, 656-0285
Krugers Korner	Outdoor Supply Co.
Absarokee 328-4475	Absarokee 328-4904

21. Camping Areas:
    Camping should be no trace, you pack it in, you pack it out. Don't leave any refuse or garbage of any kind. You do not have to camp in designated campgrounds when you are back in the Absaroka-Beartooth wilderness. You should go light but be prepared for bad weather also. It is a good idea for two people to go together in case of an accident. There is no camping allowed within 200 feet of a lake or within 100 feet of a stream. There are no rock fire rings allowed. There may be other regulations implemented from time to time. Be sure to check these before going hunting.

22. Ranger Station:
    U.S. Forest Service Ranger Station in Red Lodge - 446-2103.

23. Phone Numbers:
Montana Dept. of Fish, Wildlife & Parks in Billings - 252-4654.
Stillwater County Sheriffs Department - 1-800-736-5307.

24. Fishing:
There are Cutthroat Trout, Rainbow Trout and Eastern Brook Trout in Bighorn Sheep Area 501. There are Golden Trout and Grayling in surrounding areas.

25. Bird Hunting:
There are Blue Grouse and Ruffed Grouse in the Beartooths. The season usually opens in early September, but may change year to year, so confirm dates with Montana Fish, Wildlife, & Parks Department.

26. Maps Available:

Updated coated maps of Cooke City-Cutoff Mountain, Mount Douglas, and Mount Wood available from Rocky Mountain Surveys.
Rocky Mountain Surveys
P.O. Box 21558
Billings, MT 59104-1558
(406) 656-0366

Absarokee-Beartooth Mountains 15x30 minute quadrangle map series also available from Rocky Mountain Surveys.
Standard U.S.G.S. maps
Selby's
2595 Enterprise Avenue
Billings, Montana 59101
(406) 652-4414

Montana Highway Map

Author Note: Some information, business addresses and phone numbers may change over time.

I took this full curl bighorn ram on November 9 in the West Rosebud Canyon in Montana's Unlimited Sheep District 501. He had 35-1/2" long horns with 14-1/2" bases, scoring 163-5/8 in Safari Club Record Book. My nephew Jim Shields was with me on this hunt. The ground was covered with snow and we had already glassed a lot of country before we saw the sheep. There were my ram and two smaller ones feeding about a half a mile from us on a steep hillside. There was a slight cross wind drifting down the canyon, and I climbed, shielded by trees, to a position about 100 yards from the rams. I used my bipod for the uphill shot. This was my 4th bighorn. Bighorn sheep meat is my favorite wild meat.

HOW TO HUNT BIGHORN SHEEP IN MONTANA'S AREA 501 PART II - HUNTING STRATEGIES

You leave Billings and drive on Interstate 90 to Columbus where you turn off, go through the town of Columbus and follow Highway 78 through Absarokee to the Fishtail turnoff. From here you follow Highway 419 through Fishtail, out about 2 miles past Fishtail and then turn left on a highway that goes to Mystic Lake power plant and the West Rosebud Canyon. Follow this road to the Mystic Lake power plant. The last 14 miles is a gravel road.

Park your vehicle at the provided parking area at Mystic Lake power plant. Load your backpack and head up the trail towards Mystic Lake. Walk past Mystic Lake and Island Lake to the lower end of Silver Lake. Here you take the right hand trail up to the ridge between Storm Creek and Weeluna Lake at an elevation of 9,694 feet. This trail is indistinct and very hard to follow. You may have to just navigate cross country with your map and compass. From here climb out above and to the right of Frenco Lake along this ridge line to the plateau southwest of Twin Peaks. There are some springs here and you can camp at this location for a few days.

You are centrally located here and can glass into and across Storm Creek, Falls Creek, and Woodbine Creek. This is a good summering area for the Bighorn Sheep. Glass all day as Bighorn Sheep move at any time. I have seen rams graze all day long. Usually they will lay down in mid morning, get up to feed around noon, lay down again and then get up to feed again in mid-afternoon.

When you glass, don't just look on the open grassy plateaus but also down into the edge of the timber and in small pockets. I don't see very many Bighorn Sheep in real rocky areas, although you may catch the odd one there. They prefer grass, whether open or timbered.

Look for a dark, almost chocolate colored body, with a strikingly white rump patch. The white goes clear to the ground on a Bighorn Sheep's front and hind legs in contrast to a mule deer's white, which isn't as bright and stops at the hocks.

While here, look down into the areas below you in Falls Creek, the Stillwater River and in Storm Creek. Be careful if you try to descend into Falls Creek, Storm Creek, or Woodbine as it is very steep here and treacherous. I have walked out the bottom of Falls Creek to the Stillwater River. It is very steep but passable.

If you see sheep in Woodbine Creek, you can go back down to Weeluna Lake and over the pass into the head of Woodbine Creek. This is very wild and dangerous country, travel at your own risk. If in doubt, don't try to ascend or descend if terrain appears too rough. Know your personal limitations.

If you cannot find any sheep in this area, you can walk on through the area from Storm Mountain towards Wolf Mountain and around Sawtooth Mountain on the southside toward Inciser Lake, Little Goose Lake and back northeast toward Grasshopper Glacier. There is no trail through this area. Don't attempt it if you are not competent with maps and have ample woodsmanship ability. Go down the West Rosebud Creek to your vehicle. The trail is bad and hard to follow, sometimes non-existent down the West Rosebud Creek until you get to Silver Lake.

Another way is to leave a vehicle at the Wilderness Boundary below Goose Lake before you start your hunt and then drive out from there at the end of your hunt. You could go back around and pick up your original vehicle at Mystic Lake power plant. It could be risky to leave a vehicle at the Wilderness Boundary because it might get snowed in all winter.

This is the way to hunt this area from September 15 through October 15. After this you can make short trips into the Fishtail Plateau and other close basins as the sheep move in towards their winter range in the West Rosebud Canyon.

I suggest hunting early as the area is on a kill quota and when the quota is filled the season is closed. It is the hunter's responsibility to check to see if the season is closed. The closing date varies from year to year, depending on luck, snow, etc. You should be in good physical condition to hunt this area.

DISCLAIMER CLAUSE:
Author does not guarantee this information. Author is not responsible for errors, omissions, or information from sources deemed reliable.

Enter the Beartooth Mountains at your own risk.

I was sick in bed with the flu when some friends called and told me they had seen a ram in the sheep area where I held a tag. Dressed in my white camouflage clothing with my orange vest over that, I was glassing for the ram at dawn. I spotted the ram with a ewe and stalked it to within 150 yards. There was a 60 mile an hour cross wind blowing down the canyon. I was very sick and had perspiration running in my eyes. I missed the shot. The 4/5 curl ram ran about 600 yards and resumed feeding. I returned the next day, again found the ram, stalked him to 100 yards and shot him. The exertion broke my fever and I got better. This was my fifth bighorn ram out of the unlimited area in Montana.

I shot this antelope on October 12 near Jordan, Montana on the largest ranch in the state. The horns were 15 inches long and qualify for SCI Record Book with a score of 75-4/8 points. The state record had come off this ranch the year before. I applied for a tag in this area and after drawing it, I got permission to hunt the ranch and went to hunt as soon as the season opened there. The new state record that was killed on the ranch the year before scored over 90 Boone & Crockett points. But then we had one of the most severe winters that Montana had experienced in over 30 years. Most of the big bucks winter killed. Only healthy bucks in the prime of life and strong younger animals survived. This was the biggest buck that I could find after several days of looking. I stalked to within 125 yards of the buck as he walked through a windy pass in a high ridge. The wind was roaring at probably 70 miles per hour and I had trouble staying upright. The buck was walking broadside to me with the wind at his rear. I held my crosshairs on his hind quarters to allow for the wind drift. Wind drift all right!! I shot several feet in front of the animal and he immediately vacated. I watched him go out on the prairie near a small blue clay butte. I lined up behind the butte and again stalked to within 200 yards and dropped the buck with one shot. There was less wind here on the prairie.

Chapter 22

SULTAN OF THE PRAIRIE

The day before the season opened in early October, a friend of mine from Billings, also named Bill, set out with me to go on an antelope hunt. We loaded our gear and drove to a ranch located north of Miles City, Montana, on the Jordan road, where Bill and I had drawn permits to hunt.

We arrived at the ranch late and stopped at the house to let the ranchers know who was camping in their field. They had given us permission earlier in the summer to hunt and camp on their ranch.

We rolled out our sleeping bags near the ranch buildings and were soon asleep under the clear sky and gleaming stars.

The next morning was the first day of the pronghorn season. Our alarm clocks went off about 6:00 a.m. and we crawled out of the warm bags. A soft yellow glow was gathering on the eastern horizon as we dressed, reloaded our camp outfits, ate a couple sandwiches and drove over to the house and had coffee with the rancher. We then stored some of our excess equipment in their garage.

When there was enough light to shoot, we started out with the rancher riding along with us to point out his boundaries. We saw two herds of does and young bucks and Bill took a shot at a rapidly disappearing fox with a close miss right behind the red streak.

We drove on farther and saw several whitetail deer. We saw a total of 15 whitetails that day including 2 forkhorns and a 4 point buck. We drove by three small buck antelope on a hillside also.

After the landowner showed us his ranch boundaries, we took him back to the ranch headquarters so he could do his chores. Bill and I drove around that morning not seeing many hunters, but saw 33 antelope. We saw one large buck at long range, but was unable to get a decent shot, so we didn't shoot. We saw a few antelope in the backs of vehicles that other hunters had shot.

Around noon, Bill and I headed back to the ranch and told our friend of the scarcity of game. He suggested we hunt the rougher country to the south of his ranch where they leased grazing land. He went along to show us where the land was located. Right off we started seeing the swift prairie goats. The antelope were in small groups of 2 up to 15 head.

About mid-afternoon we saw two sizable bucks and a doe coming down a hill along a fence. We stopped and waited until they were within shooting range. Assuming a sitting position, Bill dropped the largest buck with his second shot as it ran by at top speed. The buck had nice horns, one was 16-1/4 inches long. The buck's horns scored 75 Boone & Crockett points, not a record but a nice buck anyway.

My 15 1/2 inch Antelope Buck.

We took the buck back to the ranch, hung him in a granary to cool, left the rancher to do his evening chores, and went back out again to search for a buck for me.

Bill got a shot at a coyote on a ridge and missed it also, as he had done with the fox earlier. He was using a new rifle of a different caliber than he was used to and was not accustomed to how the gun shot.

Darkness caught us on the lease land and we headed back to camp for another night, with my license still unfilled.

The next morning dawned bright and clear. We checked the ranch property without seeing any antelope so we headed back to the rough, lease land again. Bill and I saw about 125 antelope with the herds in bunches of from 15 to 25 head. We saw five large herd bucks and I shot one of these at 9:30 a.m., after a half mile run on foot to get ahead of the antelope as they moved up a draw. I lay on my stomach behind some pungent sagebrush as the animals walked into sight about 100 yards from me. Due to the clearness and brightness of the morning, the antelope's coats glistened brilliantly. At this short range, I could also see their eyes sparkle through the scope.

The buck with the high, wide flung, 15-1/2 inch horns was an easy target. I tagged him, dressed him out after picture taking, and then we returned to the ranch to pick up the other antelope.

We thanked the rancher and his wife for letting us hunt and then left for home. We arrived home about 3:00 p.m. after a very enjoyable hunt for the western sultan of the prairie, the pronghorn antelope.

This antelope buck that I shot on October 15th was a mistake. I got him northeast of Jordan, Montana in Garfield County. It had rained and the gumbo soil was slick, greasy and sticky. I was hunting on foot and would have great collections of blue mud form around my feet as I tried to traverse the countryside. I would have to stop and kick the mud off, as much as several pounds at a time. I stalked a herd of antelope with numerous good bucks in it. A satellite doe that I hadn't seen, spooked and the herd was off and running. I shot at the biggest buck, a fine 16 incher, missed him and killed this good buck that was running next in line. This big buck scored 76-3/8 SCI.

I took this buck on November 1st near Hardin, Montana. The herd was over 3/4 of a mile away when I first saw them across a big flat on the other side of a railroad track feeding in a field of winter wheat. I used a deeply cut, dry wash to cross the flat and got in behind the railroad grade to move closer to the grazing herd. It was late evening and the light was quickly slipping away. I stalked to a point directly across the track from the peaceful herd. The antelope were only about 150 yards away and undisturbed. I was easing up the grade to shoot when I herd the train whistle. Looking, I saw a freight train approaching. The engineer had apparently seen me and leaned on his horn all the way to me and past me. I tried to see under the train as it passed but couldn't see the antelope. As soon as the train from hell was gone, I looked and the field was bare, the antelope gone also. As fast as I could, I crossed the field and bellied over the rise in the middle of the undulating field. It was about the end of shooting light, but there was the herd feeding again about 50 yards from me. The biggest buck noticed me there in the short wheat and started to walk toward me. I could say I had to shoot him in self defense, but actually he was just curious or alarmed and wanted to identify what I was. He scores 80-2/8 in the Safari Club International Record Book.

152

I shot this 15-1/4 inch buck on October 19, on Pumpkin Creek between Ashland and Volberg, Montana. A taxidermist friend was hunting with me. There weren't very many antelope in this area but we located a small herd and then got permission to hunt them. The rancher said that the antelope would come down into the lower fields near the creek in late afternoon, but that they spent their days further back in the rolling sage covered hills. After several hours of searching, we located the herd that had moved again while we were talking to the rancher. We made a stalk, but it is harder for two people to do things that one person could do easily. As we were preparing to shoot on the count of three, the antelope saw us and spooked, running at a right angle to our left. My friend dropped a big buck as the group sprinted away, but I missed my shot. The herd quickly disappeared over a hill. We dressed his buck and then returned to the ranch area to let the antelope settle down and wait for the herd to come to the field in the evening. On the way in, I saw a red fox, stalked it, and shot it. I had the beautiful hide tanned. I was suffering from a bad cold and took a nap. Later, I hid myself in the field and took the largest buck as he strolled in, unaware of me. Most big game animals are creatures of habit and if you know those habits, then you can usually connect with a trophy.

6x6 Whitetail - Mule Deer Cross.

HUNTING TIPS:

Before leaving a track overnight, track a wounded animal across open ground, into the edge of cover if tracking in snow because if the wind blows, it will cover up the tracks out in the open but will not cover them as bad in the forest where there is less wind.

A wounded animal will lay down and stiffen up over night. Even if it doesn't die, it will usually be easier to see in the daylight because when they are sick, they don't hide as well.

Push a wounded animal as fast as you can if it is a lung shot because it will bleed more and die sooner, thus suffering less.

Chapter 23

WHITETAIL-MULE DEER CROSS

I can't think of any kind of big game hunting where optics are not useful. I was out one morning at daylight driving up a road into the hills from my home to hunt mule deer. I had gone about three miles when I spotted three deer walking slowly through sagebrush at the head of a canyon. They looked like they were ready to bed down for the day by the way they wandered around as they walked, as if looking for a soft place to rest until evening.

They were about 600 yards away and didn't see me as I stopped behind a small butte. I got out my spotting scope and soon could see that one was a whitetail doe, one a small whitetail buck, and one appeared to be at first glance an average size muley buck. As I watched the bigger buck, he flicked his tail out. It was long and white underneath. Now, I know that mule deer have short tails that are black tipped, but this deer had a long white one.

The big buck then laid down in foot and a half high sage brush. The doe and young buck laid down also. I put my spotting scope back into my Ford, grabbed my Husqvarna 30.06 with 3 to 9 variable Leopold scope and started my stalk. I moved unseen behind a butte to within 200 yards of where I had last seen the deer. I then crawled over the hill on my belly, inching along until I could see the bigger buck, which was bedded slightly above the other two deer. I turned the scope to 9 power and looked at the buck. He was big bodied, his color was very dark, unlike a whitetail, and his antlers stood up like a mule deer instead of sweeping forward like a whitetail.

Now, I only had one deer permit left, having shot a large buck earlier in the season. I did not want to shoot a mediocre mule deer as I have shot many mule deer and only wanted a large one. But this had to be a whitetail because my eyes had never deceived me. I had earlier seen the big white tail characteristic of that breed. I looked at the buck's head carefully as he lay unaware. Through the 9 power scope, I could see a white ring around the buck's eye and also a white line just back of the black nose separating it from the brown of the rest of the nose. These are definite whitetail deer characteristics, but the buck had a very dark skull cap, characteristic of a mule deer buck.

With the help of a strong scope, I decided that the buck was a dark colored large whitetail. I switched the scope down to 4 power, steadied on the ribcage and squeezed the trigger. I felt elated as I walked up to the buck finding him a large 6 x 6 point with about 4 or 5 inches broken off the main beam of each antler. This is part of what gave him the appearance of a mule deer besides his unusually dark color.

He was the largest whitetail (if he was a whitetail) I had taken up to that time. Without the help of the variable scope, I might have passed him up as an average mule deer buck.

I considered the buck to be a whitetail for several years, then I saw an article describing studies that had been done on crosses. The article said that the whitetail and mule deer bucks had different shaped metatarsal glands on the outside of their hind legs. The mule deer metatarsal gland is long and narrow. The whitetail metatarsal gland is round and the whitetail-mule deer cross has a metatarsal gland that is oval shaped, and mid range in size between the other two species.

I got out photos of my mystery buck and could tell by looking at it's metatarsal glands that it definitely fit the cross category. Since then I have watched for cross deer and saw a mature doe on the Boulder River near McLeod, Montana.

I saw a definite cross buck on Sage Creek in the Pryor Mountains a few years ago. The buck combined physical characteristics of both species, i.e, a rack that had whitetail deer configuration, but stood at more of an upright angle. This buck had a tail as long and big as a whitetail's, but was shaped and colored like a mule deer's. The ears were small like a whitetail also. If you know whitetail and mule deer well, these crosses are easy to pick out of a herd because of their odd combination of characteristics.

In areas where both species are found and hunted heavily, a great many of the mule deer bucks will be killed off. It seems to me that more mature whitetail bucks survive and fill in the void left by the absence of the muley bucks, and consequently do some of the breeding of the mule deer does.

Near Acton, Montana, I saw a mule deer doe and fawn and a small 2 year old 4x4 buck together one evening before the season opened. The buck had a very typical whitetail rack, a trim, sleek, whitetail body, small ears, and a big, long tail shaped like that of a mule deer. When the deer finally spooked and ran, the three all bounded away together like mule deer. They never ran, but continued bounding until out of sight. I believe that the mule deer doe was probably the buck deer's mother and its father was a pure whitetail buck.

When I was a full-time guide and outfitter, I didn't have much time to hunt on my own. I was usually either guiding hunters or scouting for game for them. Once in a while though, I would get a day or two to try to get some winter meat for myself. These days were usually the result of a hunter getting his game and leaving early. One such day, I decided to try to get a whitetail buck. That afternoon, I climbed high into a boxelder tree to watch a small clearing along Rock Creek near my home. I had been in the tree about an hour when I heard some duck hunters doing quite a bit of shooting up creek from me. I quickly climbed out of the tree and ran over towards the river where I knew there was a main game trail. I was 150 yards from the pathway, when I saw a whitetail buck running down the trail from upstream. The area between me and the trail was fairly open, except right along the trail, the young cottonwoods were as thick as a picket fence. I got into a sitting position with my Leupold scope on 9 power, and found an opening about six feet wide in the wall of trees, exposing the trail. I backed my sight picture up about ten feet into the trees, towards the way the buck was coming from. When the running buck appeared in my scope, I swung my lead ahead of him and fired into the opening, with my round catching the buck squarely in the ribs. I had collected my winter meat.

I took this 5x5 Whitetail Buck near Jordan, Montana. This is a real wide open country with a little brush along creeks and small timber patches around the waterholes. When I first saw this buck at the edge of some cottonwood timber near a reservoir, I thought he might make the Boone & Crockett Book. It took me about four seconds to judge the buck and to get him on the ground. Quick and accurate shooting will get you many more trophies in the long run. Practice shooting often. This buck had a lot smaller body and proportionally the antlers appeared bigger than they actually were. During the rut, you should hunt the doe herds. The dominant bucks will be somewhere nearby.

I shot this 4x4 Coues Whitetail Buck on November 29, in the Animas Mountains of New Mexico about two miles from the Old Mexico border. I was hunting without a guide on the 322,000 acre Gray Ranch. I paid a $500 trespass fee and took care of myself, food, camp, etc. There was an old 8"x10" log building with a concrete floor that I cleaned out in which I set up my dome tent. It had snowed and one night as I lay sleeping, I was awakened by heavy breathing and the almost imperceptible sound of an animal walking around my tent in the small building. I was wide awake now. I said "get out of here" in a strong voice. The next morning I could see the tracks of a large mountain lion in the snow.

159

Rocky Mountain Elk... high, wide, and handsome.

If you want to shoot a real trophy bull elk, take up bow hunting because you can hunt them during the rut when they are easier to locate by their bugle as they protect their herds of cows. A big bull is less wary at this time also.

Chapter 24

LONE BULL

I saw the elk herd at daylight as they wandered, grazing slowly, off the alpine Line Creek Plateau. They were going into the timber below the break of the plateau edge where they would bed for the day. I had left the camp, in the scattered pines at the head of Corral Creek, well before sunup and had ridden only a short way when I crossed the tracks the elk had made the night before in the fresh snow. I had followed them quickly in the gathering dawn and spotted the elk on the plateau rim just as they were heading into the timber. I carefully searched the herd with my spotting scope but could not see horns. I could see by the tracks that some of the elk had already gone into the timber.

It was late November and the area had been hard hunted all fall by local hunters and by nonresident hunters from an outfitter's camp. Many of the bulls in the area had been killed. The season was open for antlered bulls only with a few either sex permits issued for a late season special hunt. I was interested only in a bull, any bull because of the lateness in the season and I needed winter meat. I was an outfitter-guide at the time and this would be my only free day to hunt elk for myself.

I glassed the herd of around 25 cows and calves, again and again, in search of a horn before they faded into the timber. They had not seen me and were not disturbed. I reined the agile bay gelding around and headed back toward camp. The elk would probably be back out in the same place that evening, so I went back to camp and waited, rather than follow them into the timber.

I fed the bay some hay and oats and watered him, then tied him up for the day. I cut wood, carried water and caught up on the chores around the camp. I ate lunch and then took a nap. About 2:30 in the afternoon, I rode out again to get positioned to ambush the elk as they came out that evening to feed.

As I topped a rise where I could see the place the elk had entered the timber that morning, I stopped short. The hillside was covered with elk. I eased from the horse and leveled the spotting scope over the saddle. There were 30 cows and calves and one lone bull grazing. The elk were out feeding about two hours before they usually did. I wondered why until I looked back up the mountain behind me and could see the heavy gray clouds advancing slowly, obliterating everything from sight as they came. The elk were trying to get their bellies full before the fury of the storm covered the grass with deep snow. They were pawing through the previous night's snow to get at the grass.

I rode behind a ridge to within 250 yards of the elk and stalked another 100 yards on foot through scattered pines. I laid down in the snow for a steadier shot at the spike bull, which was grazing broadside to me. Behind the shoulder I centered the crosshairs of the Leupold scope set on 9 power and touched off the shot. The bull lunged to the right, then started to run, turning up the white hillside in the direction the cows were headed. I quickly shot five more times at him as he easily ran up the hill not appearing to be hit. As he went over the hilltop, I noticed I had broken his right front leg. I had brought seven shells with me, plenty enough I had figured to kill an elk. I was accustomed to one shot kills. I was shooting my 30.06 with 180 grain bullets, but the bullets were soft, round-nosed bullets. These bullets were made for deer, antelope and light built game, as I was to find out later.

I now counted and reconfirmed that I only had one cartridge left. I started to walk towards where I had last seen the bull elk. I now realized that the sky had darkened considerably on the 9500 foot elevation plateau. I turned and looked back the way my horse and I had come less than half an hour before. I was staring down the barrel of a storm as mean and intense as any I had ever seen. The high winds slapped the first wet snow in my face.

Then I saw the big muley buck. He was standing in a small opening along the edge of a patch of dark timber 250 yards away. He was looking at me and his heavy horns spread beyond his ears with deep symmetrical forks. He had as big a set of horns as I had seen up to that time in my short life. I was 22 years old then.

I had a dilemma now. I thought I could kill the buck with one shot and it was tempting, but I had a wounded bull elk also. The ethics of the situation demanded that I use my only remaining shell on the elk. I turned away from the large buck and never looked back again.

I quickly closed the distance to where the elk had galloped up the slope. There on the snow were large splotches of bright crimson blood.

I was following the bull faster than I should have been as I topped the crest where I had last seen the bull running away. There was the spike bull, laying broadside to me at 30 yards. I didn't expect him to have stopped this quickly. I should have sneaked over the hill and caught him unaware. We saw each other at the same time and just as I touched off my last round, holding where the skull joins the spine, he jumped to his feet with the bullet going through his throat instead.

My heart sank as the bull ran off the plateau edge into the scattered Douglas Fir. I sneaked along his track for a hundred yards and then saw him laying 50 yards ahead of me. He saw me, sprang to his feet and ran about 50 more yards and laid down again.

I leaned my rifle against a large Douglas fir tree and opened my razor sharp Boker Tree Brand pocket knife.

I was able to sneak within 50 yards of the bedded bull again before he started to get nervous. I stopped and observed him for a minute as I formed my plan. He would watch me for a little bit, then close his eyes and nod his head for about 10 seconds before he would snap awake and look at me again. He was weakening from the loss of blood. I like to kill an animal cleanly and quickly and I was suffering immensely as I watched him suffer. I hoped I could end the ordeal quickly.

Just as he closed his eyes and started to nod his head again, I charged him as fast as I could run. I was almost to him as he opened his eyes and in one quick motion was on his feet and running down the hill with me right behind him. I was going to try to hamstring him as he ran. As I was about to strike at his hamstring tendon, he glanced back and seeing me so close, he ducked to the right, turning uphill and stopped with his front quarters and head on the uphill side of a large Douglas fir. The elk's rear quarters were positioned along side the tree and downhill towards me with the tree between us, preventing the elk from seeing me.

My momentum had carried me on by the elk and the tree, but I was able to stop in a short distance and turn back to the bull.

I could see the tips of his antlers appear on one side of the tree and then the other side as he rapidly turned his head, looking for me.

There was a heavy carpet of fir needles and I quietly eased back up the hill and cut first his right hamstring tendon, with him kicking violently at me, and then his left hamstring tendon. The bull elk now had three legs rendered useless and he was thus immobilized.

I circled to the front of the adrenalin charged elk, and facing him, shook my right hand with the knife in it toward his left side. I knew what he could do to me with his saber-like horns. He lunged and horned at my hand. As he did this, I reached in and grabbed his right horn with my left hand and pinned his neck to the ground with my knee. I quickly cut a major artery at the front of his brisket and he was dead in seconds.

I had finished what I had started, the bull didn't have to suffer for several hours before dying in the middle of the night.

I was not proud of myself. I thought this was what is was probably like for a predator to kill a prey animal in nature.

Although I had killed in a primal way, I never wanted to do it this way again. Since that time, I have always carried cartridges adequate for the game and plenty of them. If I would have had the right cartridges, I would have killed the elk with my first shot. Instead the round-nosed, lead exposed bullet splattered on the elks rib and did not penetrate.

I rapidly field dressed and tagged the bull, propping it open to cool.

The snow was falling heavily now and darkness was fast approaching.

I tried to retrace my tracks but the snow had already covered them. I searched for my rifle and had almost given up when I saw it at a distance, leaning against a tree.

I shouldered the rifle and wondered if I could find my horse now. With much difficulty, I was able to return to about where I had shot from the first time. I knew I was within 250 yards of my horse. I started in the general direction I knew him to be. I wasn't sure how far I had gone, but thought I was now near where he should be tied.

The heavy wet snow covered everything, and in the thickening darkness nothing looked the same to me as it had earlier.

I felt an extreme urgency to find the horse because I was over two miles from camp in the blinding snowstorm, and the horse's instincts were my only hope of reaching camp that night.

I was starting to worry intensely when I thought I saw something in the last light that sort of looked like "maybe?" a horse. As I approached, the horse turned his head to greet me. He was humped up with his tail to the storm and was completely blanketed by the wet snow.

After untying him and brushing the snow from the saddle, I swung on and gave him his head. I snuggled down inside my down parka, pulling the drawstring on the hood close around my face.

We traveled for what seemed like an eternity and when the horse stopped walking, I got out my flashlight and turned it on. There in front of me was the feed box, tie up area, and camp.

If a horse has been hunted in an area very much, and knows the country, he will be able to take you home even in a pitch black, nighttime blizzard.

The snow had quit by morning and the day was cold and clear with a bright sun shining.

It was hard to believe that only a few hours before a person could have feared for his life on the beautiful plateau.

I took two pack horses back to the elk and after quartering it, loaded two quarters on each horse. One horse was a bronc and bucked his load off seven times in the seven miles I had to travel to reach my vehicle.

I would have winter meat and some strong memories to last a lifetime.

I shot this large, black, wild boar on a huge ranch in south Texas on a fall hunt. The pig population there was wild and free roaming. They were a cross between domestic pigs and European wild boar. The whole country was covered with mesquite brush, oak, and cactus. I enjoyed a beautiful evening, watching the strange birds and also an armadillo feeding. I was on a ground stand at the edge of a meadow. The area was covered with pig sign, tracks and rooted up ground. About dark, the boar ambled out into the meadow and after looking around briefly, started to feed. The distance was about 150 yards and with my Leupold variable scope turned down to three power, I took an aim on the boar and waited until he turned broadside. At the lung shot, the boar bolted and ran back into the brush the way he had come from earlier. I listened carefully with my hands cupped behind my ears and heard the pig as he went down and briefly thrashed the brush. I pinpointed his location by the noise and walked straight to him, approaching carefully, but I could see he was already dead. I had the meat made into steaks and hot mexican sausage in San Antonio. It was excellent. I went from here to west Texas where I hunted whitetail deer on another large ranch, where the game was also wild and free roaming. I appreciate the wilder parts of Texas, and have hunted there several times.

I got this fine Whitetail Buck on December 18, in west Texas' Kinney County. The buck easily makes Safari Club International's Record Book. A friend from Montana and myself were hunting a 15,000 acre ranch that didn't allow many hunters. We tried horn rattling, still hunting, and stand hunting. To be successful at stand hunting you have to shift down a couple of gears from today's active life and harmonize with nature. If you find peace within yourself, you can set a stand much easier and longer. It was hot and dry and nothing was working. Then a norther blew in, the temperature dropped to 15 degrees above zero and a cold rain started to fall. I was out by daylight the next cold morning. The rain had quit, the sun was shining and there were deer moving everywhere. I shot the pictured buck right off that morning. My friend shot a nice heavy horned buck. Whitetail bucks are one of my favorite animals to hunt, probably because of the challenge of outsmarting these outdoor Einsteins. Whitetail bucks are one of God's most graceful and beautiful animals, a joy to see, a jewel to collect and cherish. I hunt big whitetail bucks by still hunting, trail watching, scrape watching, horn rattling, making drives, using a grunt call, glassing large areas, and floating rivers. How ever you hunt them, they are always interesting, exciting, and a real kick.

166

I got this, my second Javelina, on the same west Texas hunt as the whitetail buck. I had already taken the buck and was headed out to retrieve a stand when I bumped into this old boar. I 30-06ed him as he ran up a draw ahead of me. I laid him in some shade and continued on up the draw to get the stand. I returned shortly and this gray fox was sniffing of my javelina. The fox saw me and ran up on a hillside, stopping broadside in some brush 175 yards away. I chambered a solid military round and shooting from a prone position, dropped him with a lung shot. Javelina have poor eyesight but have excellent hearing and sense of smell. They can see you at close range if you move and will flee rapidly. Javelina are a herding animal and of the four that I have shot, only this west Texas boar was alone. I have noticed that the big old boars' bodies look chunkier and fuller than the other younger or female pigs. The old boars I have experience with have a yellowy looking appearance, compared to the darker females and younger javelina. A boar's head also looks long from nose tip to back of the ears. The old boar's head also appears deep from top to bottom on a side view. My second largest javelina is a female with a giant body and an extra long skull. Females can be big too. When javelina are alarmed or annoyed, they clack their teeth together making a loud, threatening noise.

T.S. Bateman

I dearly love the Arizona desert. I shot this, my first, Javelina in February of 1969 when I was 23 years old. My brother Doug and I traveled to Tucson to spend a couple of months away from the cold winter of Montana. I was using a borrowed 7mm Mag with 139 grain hollow points. I almost never fall down in Montana, but fell a couple of times a day on the very unstable volcanic rock of the Sahuarita Mountains. I went out hunting with some members of a predator calling club and shot coyote, gray fox, and bobcat. They asked me if I wanted to go javelina hunting and I readily accepted. We drove to the edge of the mountains and then separated and hunted on foot. Everything in the desert has thorns. In the photo you can see the long stalked ocotillo, flat bladed prickly pear cactus, and the big saguaro cactus with its mighty arms. Some saguaro cactus live to be 150 years old. I saw desert mule deer, a fine 4x4 coues whitetail buck, blacktailed jackrabbits, and many exotic birds. There would be frost in the morning but then about midmorning the southwestern sun would warm the air and it would be beautiful hunting for the rest of the day. A chill would come on just after the sun set in the evenings. I shot my javelina on the second day of hunting and Doug got one later. If you field dress the javelina first, before taking off the scent glands, the meat will be much better.

169

I took my first Javelina in Arizona. I also shot my 4th Javelina on February 21, 1992, in the Chiricahua Mountains of eastern Arizona. My wife, Diana, and I decided to spend a working holiday in Tucson for 2-1/2 months, so she got a leave of absence from her job and we headed south. There were some excess javelina tags available and I applied for and got one. The night before the season opened, I drove from Tucson to the Chiricahua Mountains and camped. I got permission to hunt on a large ranch on the east face of the mountains. After hunting only 6 hours of the first day, I shot this long tusked boar that scores 14-10/16 SCI and is #7 in the world. It also makes the Arizona Record Book.

Chapter 25

TRAINING THE HUNTING HORSE

I have been around horses most of my life. My parents have had various ranches and when I was growing up I always had a horse or two. When I was very young, during my first few years of school, I would spend part of each summer in a cow camp on the Crow Indian Reservation with my grandad where he punched cattle for the cattlemen's association. It was here that I learned my basic horsemanship.

I traded a very good bicycle for a 3 year old unbroken mare when I was in the seventh grade. With the help of my father and a couple of local ranchers, who had moved here from Texas long ago and were real cowboys, I broke that mare. Since then I have had and broken many horses especially during high school to make spending money. I used many of them hunting and I outfitted non-resident hunters for several years using many horses in the mountains around hunting camps.

A good trained horse is a joy to hunt with and is indispensible for back country hunting for large animals such as moose and elk. A good hunting horse can almost never be purchased. If someone has one, they don't want to sell it. If you can buy a hunting horse it usually has a few faults which are the reasons it is for sale. Some of these horses are fairly good but are either old or have one or more bothersome bad habits.

The best way to get a hunting horse that will pack or ride, one you can shoot around, and one that is gentle and dependable is to buy a colt and raise and train him the way you want him. I like quarter horses but many good mountain hunting horses are of questionable ancestry.

Once you have acquired a colt (the younger and unspoiled the better) you can go to work training him immediately. Gentle him and gain his confidence. Never mistreat him; train him slowly, methodically so he learns his lessons well. Through much repetition in daily lessons I teach a colt to come to a whistle, to be caught easily, to not spook at rattling equipment or flopping things that he will encounter later, and to let me pick up his feet easily so he won't be hard to shoe.

To train him to be unafraid of gunfire and loud noises, I start shooting a .22 rifle around him, first at a distance then up closer. I then increase the caliber until I can shoot a big game rifle near him without exciting him.

I get him used to hobbles, then I train him so that I can rope off of him in case I need to use him for wrangling other horses.

Break your colt to pack anything. Sacks of pop cans are good to get a horse used to a rattling pack. Sacking out can be used on horses that are

171

afraid of flopping things which they will eventually encounter when the wind blows their pack covers. Sacking out consists of tying up a foot so the horse cannot escape, and then slapping him with an old sack until he will stand without spooking, realizing that a flopping cloth will not hurt him.

Work with him until he loads well in a trailer or truck since you will have to transport him to the hunting area and don't want to have to fight him each time you load him.

Train him to stand while tied so that you can leave him for long periods while you hunt on foot. Get him in good physical condition and you are ready to go to the mountains for the fall.

4 x 5 mule deer buck taken by Diana Butler on November 6, 1997. We used an irrigation canal to stalk within 29 yards of the buck as he lay in his bed under a Russian Olive overhang. Diana took the buck with one shot from my 30.06 Husqvarna.

I am fascinated with nature and with wild animals in particular. Maybe that's why I appreciate well done, lifelike taxidermy so much. I believe good specimens should be preserved for others to see and enjoy not just aesthetically but for educational purposes also. I know of several trophy hunters who have donated their collections to colleges or museums allowing other people the chance to view an exotic species or a supreme example of a native species. I have seen and studied many thousands of head of live wild game in my life and am also familiar with anatomy. I have started doing my own taxidermy because I want to capture some of the unique features I have observed in the wild.

173

I shot this wild turkey in the Ekalaka Hills in eastern Montana on April 18. This was my second wild turkey ever, a big jake. The spring day was warm and gentle and my wife was with me. We weren't familiar with the area, so we started by glassing along a timber edge. We had searched only a short time when Diana, who was inexperienced at turkey hunting, asked me if that "black thing" about 300 yards from us was a turkey. I looked and sure enough it was a lone turkey headed our way. I hid myself ahead of the jake on a ponderosa pine covered ridge and ambushed it as it walked in front of me. I used a solid point military bullet in my 30-06 so I wouldn't damage the turkey unnecessarily.

On April 15, the first day of the season, I shot this 20 lb. turkey with a 9-1/2" beard in eastern Montana. I was looking for a camp site near dark, just after my wife and I arrived in the area. I spotted four toms and five hens at half a mile with my naked eye. We stalked them and I shot the gobbler with the longest beard. At the shot, two toms closest to the one I shot, jumped him and started pecking and scratching at the tom as he flopped around. One gobbler started strutting, and only left when I walked out of a finger of ponderosa pine, toward them. There was an antelope buck laying within 10 feet of the tom when I shot. I scared him pretty good. We returned home that same night.

A hunting buddy and I were camped on the Custer National Forest in eastern Montana. About dark, I heard a flock of turkeys go to roost and I marked the location for the next morning's hunt. On the morning of September 17th, we were near the ponderosa pine trees at daylight, but the flock had already flown down. We circled ahead of them but they had passed before we got into position. Turkeys sometimes move fairly fast while feeding. We started stalking the turkeys from behind, as they would go out of sight over a ridge. This way we were able to get close enough for a shot. My friend shot a jake and I shot a hen that I thought was a jake. I was still learning about turkeys. This was my 5th.

April 10th, Choccolocco Wildlife Management Area, Alabama, 60 degrees at 5:00 a.m.
My cousin, Scott Butler and myself were on our fourth day of turkey hunting before we
got a gobbler to answer. He was down a ridge from us about 200 yards away. We moved
75 yards closer and set up with Scott ten yards behind me. The turkey would gobble
every time Scott called. I saw the turkey drumming and strutting. When he came closer,
I held the gold bead sight at the base of his neck and at the shot, the gobbler flipped end
over end for about five yards. He weighed 19 pounds and had a 10-3/8" beard. This was
my sixth wild turkey, and my first Eastern wild turkey. This was my first turkey with a
shotgun. INTENSE!

April 21st, Jordan Montana. The big gobbler came off the roost at 5:55 a.m. I had already been hiding and waiting for 40 minutes, having arrived in the dark. I was well camouflaged as I called to the tom on my Lynch box call. He would not leave his flock of hens, but a jake circled behind me and then returned to the group. Another big gobbler was calling and approaching from down the draw. My first bunch of turkeys fed behind a small butte, heading for the other tom. When they were out of sight, I moved between the two gobbler's paths of travel and hid myself. I took the original tom at 25 yards with my 12 gauge shotgun. He had a 9-1/4" beard, weighed 18 pounds, and was my 7th wild turkey.

September 2, Jordan, Montana. Diana took this big Merriams wild turkey hen with my .223 Winchester Featherweight rifle, the first morning of our hunt. It was an extremely hot, dry day and we wore snake leggings for protection from rattlesnakes. She shot the turkey from a ground stand as it walked by at 50 yards. She had been sick in bed with a bad cold but came out and hunted just long enough to shoot her first wild turkey. Diana then returned to the travel trailer to wear out the virus. We ate the turkey for Thanksgiving dinner and it was delicious. We hunt turkeys in the fall with small caliber rifles and use shotguns for the spring hunt when gobblers can be called.

September 3, Jordan, Montana. Same hunt as last photo. My brother Jim, his wife, Judy and their sons Reese and Brad were along on this hunt also. We helped the boys get their first wild turkeys. I stalked three gobblers in some tall grass near a ravine. When I peeked over the edge of the ravine at 25 yards, the feeding turkeys dropped to the ground and held perfectly still for 45 minutes. The two younger toms then resumed feeding with me waiting, with the safety off, for the old veteran. Even though I hadn't moved, the old timer hadn't forgotten about me. He came up running and I missed my shot with the .223 rifle. Later that day I did get him. My eighth wild turkey. He weighed 17 lbs. and had a 9" beard.

November 24, 1991, Custer National Forest, Montana. I left camp at about 4 o'clock in the evening and hunted up a long, ponderosa pine covered canyon for about 2 miles. I came out at the upper end to the edge of a sizable, grassy plateau. I could see a large bunch of turkeys feeding toward the timber at 400 yards. I returned to the cover of the canyon and moved to intercept them. As I sneaked to the edge of the timber again, in the weakening daylight, I could see some turkeys coming towards me at 40 yards across the snow covered ground. I used my 10 power Zeiss binoculars to find the tom with the longest beard. I put the glasses down and got on him with my .223. Just as he came broadside through a little 1-1/2 foot wide opening in the scattered juniper and pines, my quick shot put him down. He was my ninth wild turkey weighing 18 lbs. with an 8-3/4" beard. I had a second turkey tag good for the fall season, so about dawn the next morning I went back out again. With my glasses, I spotted 33 turkeys at over a half a mile away as they fed over the skyline. I tracked the turkeys throughout the day, stalking ahead of them, concealing myself, then letting them wander by. Late that evening, I shot the one with the longest beard, a hen with a 7" beard, my tenth turkey. She fooled me. Hens are legal in the fall. My King of the Mountain camouflage wool clothing works great on turkeys.

April 30, 1992, Carbon County, Montana. Special permit draw area. I scouted this flock of turkeys before season. I knew this tom was the biggest and hunted him several times over a 20 day period. As you can see from the photo, I sometimes wear different camouflage patterns together, which helps to break up my image better. This gobbler had one hen with him and wouldn't come to my diaphragm call. I stalked him along the edge of a plateau, only moving when I was sure he was over the ridge and out of sight. I called all the while and stalked to within 10 yards before inching over the rise and taking him with one shot from my 12 gauge. Turkey number 11. Weight 20 lbs., beard 10".

Chapter 26

A Real Fish Story

I think it all started when we were young boys - my brother being a better fisherman than me that is. When Doug and I were lads my father would take us fishing. He would take the whole family and we would fish during the day and in the evening we would have a picnic. We fished in the mountains, along foothill streams and even in the slow moving Yellowstone and Clark's Fork rivers near home.

I never cared much for fishing and after a little while without a bite would reel in my worms (that was before I found out that fish would try to eat metal, rubber, yarn, and deer hair also). I would set my pole against a tree and start scouting around. I had much more fun doing this than I did sitting waiting for a fish to bite. Later, when I got a .22 rifle, I would hunt for something that I could see, rather than try to catch a fish that might be at the other end of the lake from where I was fishing.

All this time Doug kept fishing. He was lucky at it and had learned a lot from experience. He would always catch his limit. But I didn't care if he caught more fish than I did, as long as he caught enough for us both to eat.

We went to a fish derby one day in August, the summer after I had graduated from high school. We thought one of us might be lucky enough to win. Doug needed a pickup to run his trapline with that winter, and I needed money for college where I planned to major in rodeo with a minor in girl watching. There was a $1000 first prize for the largest fish caught.

That morning, while testing the current's drift, Doug caught a 27 pound brown trout on an empty hook and quit fishing. I kept trying but couldn't capture anything. Little kids were catching fish, old ladies were catching fish, a dog even ran into the water and pulled out a nice rainbow. All this time I sat without a bite. The little kids laughed at me, the old ladies said they were sorry I didn't catch any, and the mongrel dog brought his fish over and offered it to me.

My brother easily won the derby. I was embarrassed, humiliated, ashamed, and also changed. I was determined to out-fish my brother!

That fall when I entered college, I went to the famed Rocky Mountain Fishing Institute in Timbukto, Montana. I went there four years earning a Bachelor's degree in General Fishing with a minor in Fly Tying. I went on for a Master's degree in Trout Fishing Techniques. I then changed to Eastern Montana Fish College where I received my Doctorate in Ictheology. Now I was ready.

I challenged my brother to a fishing contest. I was confident and ready with my new knowledge and my expensive equipment. Doug just used

9 lb. Alaskan Rainbow Trout

a cane pole with a worm. We went down to a stream near home and Doug caught his limit of everything legal about as fast as he could pull them in. He then went home and I sat there all day, through the hot sun, and into the night.

I tried everything I had learned without so much as a nibble. About midnight I called it quits, threw my creel into the water, broke my pole, threw it in also and started to stomp off up the bank. About this time I heard a deep voice call from the stream. I stopped and looked toward the water. There in the middle silhouetted against the moonlight was the biggest trout I had ever seen, with his head sticking out of the water. He eyed me casually and said, "When you get to the house be sure and tell your brother to come back tomorrow."

In October this past fall, I accompanied a friend to a Wyoming lake to fish for Snake River Cutthroat Trout. I bought a one-day license for $5.00. We fished for several hours with him catching two 5 pounders, and me catching nothing. What I lack in skill, I make up for in perseverance. I bought another $5.00 license and returned the next day. My friend and I fished for several more hours on a cold, windy day, with me finally catching a stocky 5 pounder. The Snake River Cutthroat was peach colored with black speckles covering most of him. The superb fish had the telltale orange cutthroat markings under its jaw. I had the fish mounted so others can enjoy its beauty also.

One fall, I had a bush pilot fly me out of King Salmon, Alaska, and drop me off, by myself, down the Alaska Peninsula, past the Cinder River, on the north side of the Aleutian Range to hunt caribou. After several days of eating dehydrated food, I decided I wanted some fresh meat. There was a small stream, about five feet wide, that wound its way up from Bristol Bay and right past my camp. The salmon were running upstream to spawn and I had no trouble catching a 12 pound male. I completely ate him in two days. I buried the bones a great distance from my camp, because I had seen eleven Alaskan brown bears within a half mile of my camp and didn't want to attract them to me. I hunted daily in the misty rain, seeing over 500 caribou with many big bulls, but did not see any exceptional trophy bulls that I would shoot. I have hunted Alaska three times, only shooting game on the last trip. I will not shoot an inferior animal just to have one of that specie, but will try to return on another hunt to collect a genuine trophy. To me, this is better conservation than letting my ego force me to just fill my tag and bring home something, so I won't look bad to other hunters. True trophy hunting is the best method of conservation of game animals. You only take the old that are going to die soon anyway, and have already left their genetic mark on their specie.

Chapter 27

CHOOSING AN OUTFITTER FOR TROPHY GAME

The outfitter's camp sat in a secluded meadow park in a small sheltered canyon, covered like a blanket, with climax Douglas fir. A dirt road snaked through the timber to the camp, located only a couple of miles from a main gravel road. The camp was orderly, arranged, with a large cook tent, equipped with a propane cooking stove, refrigerator, and Coleman lanterns for light. There was a large mess tent with permanent tables for eating and used for nothing else. Behind and slightly up the hill were large sleeping tents, spaced for privacy. They had heavy metal, wood burning stoves and permanent bunks built into them that remained year round, even when the outfitter had moved the rest of his gear back to civilization for another ten months. There was a tent for gear and miscellaneous other camp needed things like chainsaws, tire chains, block and tackles, extra propane bottles, lantern gas, tools, and a million and one other things that might be needed.

The camp hunted with a fleet of open topped jeeps along the many driveable trails and county roads that laced this part of the mountains. The food was excellent, prepared three times a day by the outfitter's wife. The comradery was great, with the outfitter holding the dudes spellbound for a couple of hours each night after supper with his considerable tales of past hunts, some true, some not so true.

In the mornings, we would rise way before sunup, eat a breakfast of pancakes, real butter, choice of syrups, karo or maple, bacon, ham, eggs, hashbrowns, coffee and orange juice. We would then go out to hunt and come back in for lunch around noon or before. Then, after lunch the hunters would take a nap while the guides cut wood, restocked the wood in the tents, refueled lanterns, and any other chores that needed to be done.

In late afternoon the hunters would be summoned from their tents by the guides and go off in different directions for the evening hunt. We would arrive back at camp shortly after dark to a very hearty, many course, dinner while the clients and guides retold of the day's adventures.

The game pole usually gained another carcass or two each day, mostly forkhorned muley bucks, and later in the season when the rut got going, a few larger bucks, but not many. The five week seasons take on elk rarely exceeded four bulls total, which were usually young spikes, and

I shot this giant Stone sheep on October 17 in upper British Columbia, Canada with outfitter Red Sorensen. The ram was the largest Stone sheep taken in North America that year. It was number three in Safari Club International and was high in Boone & Crockett also. The exceptional ram scores 175 Boone and Crockett points, with a 42 inch curl and heavy horns. The ram has a black body and a silver face. I have it lifesize mounted, laying down. Red Sorensen ran a well organized camp in a game rich area. His guides showed exceptional hunting skills and guided for Stone sheep, Canada moose, mountain goat, grizzly bear, mountain caribou and wolves. The day before I shot this sheep, we had seen a 9 foot grizzly feeding on the mountainside above us. I couldn't shoot him since I didn't have a grizzly bear tag so we detoured around the big bear. The day I got this ram, we had ridden horseback up a large side canyon. We spotted several Stone sheep ewes and lambs that we passed underneath of in the beautiful drainage. The young guide and I tied our horses up and climbed about a quarter of a mile on up the canyon. We were glassing when we heard something running behind us. I rolled to my stomach and waited with my rifle ready as a 37 incher and my ram came out of some bushes and stopped broadside at 25 yards. I easily collected a true trophy with one shot from my 30-06.

four and five points with an occasional small six pointer. The outfitter advertised black bear hunting also in his brochures, but as far as I know, there has never been one taken from this camp.

This kind of hunt is great for older hunters, soft hunters, family groups, who only want an outing, pleasant and comfortable. It is also good for inexperienced hunters, first time out west, who don't know what to look for, but have to start somewhere. At least this hunt will give them perspective to judge other outfitters and hunts by.

I worked for another outfitter/guide at this camp in the 60's. It was great fun for the young man that I was and I learned many things about outfitting and people. There was not a lot of game taken and almost no trophy game, because the area had too many roads, was too accessible to the hordes of other hunters which we could not get away from, and the game was harvested closely each year, not allowing for any trophy growth.

I have shared this camp and outfitting operation with you to show you what not to do if you desire to hang a true trophy head on your wall.

Access is the first consideration in picking an outfitter. If the outfitter has an exclusive state guide area that no other outfitter can use, then that is the first step. The area should be remote enough that the locals cannot get to it easily either. An alternative to an exclusive government guide area is a private ranch hunt where the game is managed for quality and not over harvested.

Another case is a public area where game is managed for trophy hunts. Several states do this with many different animals successfully. Examples are four point or better or limited entry draw hunts on mule deer bucks, branch antlered or sometimes 5 points only or above on elk as in Oregon, 3/4 curl on bighorn sheep in Montana, 4/5 curl on bighorn sheep in Alberta, full curl on Dall sheep in Alaska, or more technical yet, in Nevada a 6 year old desert bighorn ram or one that scores 144 points by the Boone & Crockett system. All members of this hunt have to go through an indoctrination class put on by the Nevada Game and Fish Department.

Even if an outfitter is set up in an area, and the animals are able to reach the age necessary to grow large racks or bodies, because of either remoteness, government control of seasons, or private ranch management for older age animals, this still does not mean there will be record class game. A trophy is in the eye of the beholder, but record class is established by certain guidelines and requirements set up by different record keeping bodies. Examples are the Boone and Crockett Club, Pope and Young Club, for bow killed trophies, and Safari Club International, a record book that covers all the different game animals of the world.

This is a Quebec Labrador Caribou that I took near Schefferville in northern Quebec on September 24. This was a real enjoyable hunt. The terrain was gently rolling, with lakes in every direction and some brush cover. I saw as many as 150 bulls per day. I had only one tag and passed bigger bulls than the one that I finally shot. My rifle was lost in transit for the first three days of a five day hunt. I borrowed a guide's rifle, and you could only see clearly to 50 yards through the blurry rifle scope. A giant Boone & Crockett bull came by at 200 yards and I couldn't even shoot. My rifle arrived on the fourth day and I shot this double shovel bull that makes Safari Club's Record Book

The second step for an outfitter to produce trophy animals is genetics.

An animal, to qualify for the records, has to have the genetics to grow large antlers, horns, or skulls. Age alone will not do this. In every area, even areas with genetically inferior animals, there are from time to time animals that show up that make the record books. These are either throwbacks to an earlier genetic superiority from a recessive gene or are mutants of something new. You want to hunt an area that has historically produced quality animals, not an area that produces one animal of quality every fifty years. These are freaks of nature. You can figure these areas out by studying the record books.

An example of quality versus quantity is the black bear of Montana. Montana black bears grow fairly large but the skulls do not seem to get as large as in other areas outside Montana. There are just a few black bears that qualify for the Boone & Crockett Club that have ever been killed in Montana. That is only a few out of all the black bears that have ever been taken in Montana. One the other hand, Saskatchewan to the north of us has some taken every year. I saw two Boone & Crockett bears taken out of one Saskatchewan camp on one hunt. Southern Wyoming produces record class bears as does Idaho, Colorado, Arizona and last but not least is Utah, with not many bears, but the world record is a picked up skull from San Pete County there. British Columbia, mostly along the coast, comes up with a fair share of big black bears as does southeast Alaska. Interior Alaska produces almost no Boone & Crockett black bears.

This is just one example of a species' quality.

Okay, we now have an area that the animals get old enough to grow large trophy proportions, also with a good genetic. This, as I said, can be ascertained from studying the record books. Now we have to find a guide, unless you want to go hunt on your own, but that is a whole other story, what this book is mostly about.

All guides and outfitters are as different from each other as any two people anywhere. I personally don't care what an outfitter is like as a man because I can stand just about anybody for the length of a hunt. What I care about is not whether he is a nice guy, but does he produce quality trophies consistently. If the outfitter gets good game year after year, people will know. Safari Club International's record book lists the guide as well as the hunter. The guide is the one that deserves most of the true credit for the trophy anyway. A hunter comes and spends a few days and then goes back to his job. He has to be in fairly good shape, be able to shoot fairly well, and should be able to take orders. Many hunters can't take orders very well and lose many trophies each year because they ignored the guides' expert advice in a clutch situation. If the outfitter is as experienced as your research has shown him to be, then do

191

what he tells you and you will add more trophies to your wall.

Please don't misunderstand me here. I enjoy my hunts very much. Whether after meat or a trophy animal, a hunter gets out of a hunt what he puts into it. I appreciate the saffron dawns, the flaming sunsets, the mist in the valley, the sunlight, the new snow, the exercise, the brisk air, and the sun on a buck's horns. Some think that a trophy hunter is only a machine that enjoys only adding more numbers to his tally. I know many top trophy hunters and they are all individuals who enjoy much more about a hunt than just the kill.

Back to picking an outfitter. An outfitter that produces trophy game will have pictures of kills in the field with him or his guides in the pictures. If he only has a couple of pictures of trophy game and he is noticeably younger in the picture, then watch out.

Most importantly, the good outfitter will have good references. People who were successful as well as those who didn't get game. Sometimes an unsuccessful hunter won't take the blame for his own short comings in not getting his trophy such as poor shooting, poor physical condition, not following directions, etc. He may falsely give a bad report on the outfitter because of his own injured ego and has to have a scapegoat. You can get around this guy by talking to several different references.

A hunter's chances of taking an outsize trophy are greatly increased when he hunts with a top guide.

Good hunts aren't cheap. You can go on several low priced hunts and still not collect a trophy or you can go on one real good hunt with a top outfitter and most likely get your prized animal. There are no guarantees in hunting, but there most definitely are odds to play when choosing an outfitter.

Trophy hunts are usually of longer duration than regular hunts also.

One of the most important things to consider when booking with an outfitter is whether or not he is law abiding. Some outfitters produce big trophies by breaking the law. Outfitters who obtain trophies for clients by unlawful means should be avoided at all cost.

Go attend some hunter conventions. I have attended as many as six per year since 1975, such as the Foundation for North American Wild Sheep, Safari Club International, and the Rocky Mountain Elk Foundation to name a few. Meet the guides in person, see their photos, videos, and trophies. Some of their former clients will probably be in attendance. Talk to these hunters and these clients may tell you of other clients to contact. Get a first hand feel for the guide-outfitter, then make up your mind.

I don't care personally if the tent leaks, if there is too much salt in the food, and my bed is made on a rock, if the outfitter is crude, crabby, or

Quebec Labrador Caribou Bulls

quiet as long as he is dedicated to taking trophy game for his hunters. He's the man for me. I can still enjoy the outdoors just as much, the wilds are a constant, changed only by the seasons.

Although I was an outfitter-guide for over 20 years, I have only been on a half a dozen guided hunts in my life, where I was the hunter. Most of these hunts were extremely enjoyable. I would go on more if I could afford it.

In some states and provinces, you are not allowed to hunt on your own for certain species and having a guide is required.

Even for the species that you can hunt on your own, it will take some time to become proficient enough for you to take trophy game regularly.

I enthusiastically recommend that you go on some self-guided hunts. This is where you will challenge yourself and really learn how to hunt.

Go on some guided hunts too though, as you can spare time and money for them. You will see new country and probably learn new hunting techniques because every outfitter-guide is a unique individual and has his own way of hunting.

I hope you get the trophy of your lifetime.

This Southeastern Spanish Ibex is number 18 in Safari Club International Record Book. It has 26-1/2 inch long horns with 9-1/4 inch bases. I hunted it in the Sierra Nevada Mountains in southeastern Spain, they are big, wild mountains like we have in North America. The nearest town was Granada. I walked 13 miles the first day and saw 50 ibex, passing up a fairly good one. That night I had a exotic dinner of prawns, octopus and baby eels. December 13 dawned bright and clear. The cool dry day reminded me of Montana. We spotted the large ibex in the evening as he come down to a stream to water. I shot him there and by the time we got to him it was dark and we had to use the flash for a photo.

December 14. Still in Spain. The next day we drove from Granada to Malaga, where I saw the Mediterranean Sea for the first time. We drove on to San Roque and at one place could see Morocco in northern Africa across the china blue Mediterranean Sea. I also saw the Rock of Gibraltar here. Our destination was a large well cared for ranch. After lunch, myself and the guide went up into some rough country to hunt mouflon sheep. I saw a very good red stag and also a real big fallow buck. We spotted a herd of mouflon sheep near the crest of a ridge line, and after a circuitous stalk, I peeked over and shot the largest ram at 25 yards, just before dark. My guide was Paco.

December 17. My hunt in Spain was with Cazatur which is owned by Ricardo Medem. They run a first class outfit and get good trophies for their hunters. Our next stop would be Mr. Medem's private hunting ranch, a sprawling, brush and tree covered 20,000 acre spread called El Castano. We will hunt Spanish Red Stag and European Wild Boar. The second day of hunting we saw 100 red deer, one a 20 point stag, but we couldn't get a shot. That night, after dinner, I went on stand at the edge of a meadow and shot a wild boar in the moonlight. This is how they hunt the nocturnal boars. In Spain, the ranchers own the game, and sell the harvested meat just like ranchers do cattle in America.

December 20. I got in on a traditional Spanish Monteria which consisted of 500 dogs of all types, and handlers pushing wild boar across cut lines to standing hunters. It was a gorgeous, foggy, rainy, overcast day and I saw a lot of red deer, but no boar. I didn't shoot anything. The Monteria was followed by a feast and party. I met the head of the Bulgarian Game Department and also some of Spain's top wildlife officials. December 21 - My new guide Cresencio is 53 years old and has been on this ranch all of his life. We hunted stag this day and in the evening, went on stand for boar from 8 p.m. to 4 a.m., finally shooting an extremely large boar. I smelled it before I saw it.

Cresencio can't speak English and I speak only a little Spanish, but we both speak the universal language of the hunter. We were as in tune with each other as two hunting wolves following their instincts. December 23, Cresencio made a drive and drove 25 stags out past me. One was of gold medal class, but I couldn't get a shot. Just at dusk, I saw a large stag skylined at 300 yards facing me. I pointed it out to Cresencio and he barked "Oro" meaning gold medal, then excitedly "shoot hombre, shoot". I shot twice, hitting the stag both times, bringing it down. The stag was a 7x8, scoring 222 points. It was number 3 in the Safari Club International Record Book when I shot it.

I took this Persian Ibex, which is native to Asia, on a western game ranch in a 20 square mile pasture. The ibex herd had been free roaming there for 15 years and were extremely wild. To me, ibex are a regal animal with their flowing coats and sweeping horns. This billy had 36-1/4" long horns with 9-1/4" bases and scored 91 in Safari Club's Record Book. You hunt them like mountain goats or sheep with a lot of glassing and then stalking. They are herd animals found in large groups, including the mature billys. I made a 150 yard lung shot with my 30-06. I like ibex and would like to hunt other species of them in their native lands. They make an interesting and unusual trophy.

I took this Catalina Goat on the same west Texas hunt that I took my aoudad ram on, in the Davis Mountains. My wife, Diana, and I accompanied the guide and we climbed high on the rocky, mountainside. We had climbed up through the snow on the west face, and then circled around to the south face where the snow had melted, spotting a herd of goats in the exquisite rugged terrain. The goats had spotted us and were moving off through the jumble of boulders and cliffs. I quickly picked what I thought was the biggest billy and angled a 180 grain pointed soft point bullet through his rib cage. The black and white billy had attractive, wide flaring horns. We were dressed in wool and down clothing.

The day after I took the Catalina Goat, myself, the guide and another hunter, went out into the desert foothills to hunt for javelina. We were on a rocky outcropping overlooking a grassy bottom. This would be our evening stand. The shadows were lengthening as a herd of javelina wandered out into the clearing. I had told the other hunter that he could have the first shot. He missed the 150 yard shot with his chosen pig running to the right. A large pig came out of the bushes on the left and I anchored it with one shot. My friend continued to shoot at his running pig but was unable to get it. My javelina was #7 in SCI Record Book at the time, with a skull measurement score of 14-6/16. It currently ranks number 11.

Aoudad ram taken in the 7000 foot Davis Mountains of west Texas in January. This ram had 27 inch long horns and the bases were extremely heavy at 13-1/2 inches. The official SCI score is 134-3/8. It snowed while we were there and the temperature stayed below freezing. Thirty-five aoudad sheep pinned us down on a windy, rock knob and intermittently fed towards us over a five hour period. Five smaller rams stood sentinel while the monarch would sleep. I was shaking so bad from the cold that I had to let the sheep approach to a 100 yards before I was confident of my shot, finally taking the largest ram. These sheep were transplanted here over 20 years ago and are free roaming with no game proof fencing.

Chapter 28

TROPHY BULLS OF THE BLACK HILLS
A HUNT FOR A
BOONE & CROCKETT BUFFALO

Reprinted by permission from Boone & Crockett Club Associates Newsletter, November 1989.

On January 27, 1986, a Monday, I returned to Billings, Montana, from Las Vegas, Nevada where I had been attending the annual convention of Safari Club International. I flew on Western Airlines arriving home at 11:30 p.m. Today is my birthday!

In the morning, Tuesday the 28, my brother, Jim, and I got our gear together and left Billings by 1:45 p.m. We followed Interstate 90 through Sheridan, Buffalo, and Gillette, Wyoming, turning southeast at Moorcroft on Highway 16 to Custer, South Dakota. From Custer out to Custer State Park we took 16A. We camped in Jim's camper trailer at Grace Coolidge Campground. We went to bed at 10:00 p.m. under clear skies.

January 29, Wednesday.

We arose with excited expectations at 6:30 a.m. We had breakfast, loaded the pickup, and drove the short one and one-half miles to Custer State Park headquarters.

The terrain is granite hills and canyons with rolling plains to the east. The hills are covered with ponderosa pine trees. There are quaken aspen along the bottoms of the creeks and also some small oaks. There are some swampy areas with cattails and bog grass.

I got my $2.00 hunting license from South Dakota and paid $1800 for the buffalo hunt. Here we met Fred, the guide, about 8:00 a.m. He will guide me on my hunt. He has been the buffalo manager for 30 years, and knows the area well. The 68 year old man is from Waco, Texas originally, and used to ride bulls in rodeos and belonged to the Turtle Association. Fred is married, has 4 children that have left home, and he lives on the state park. He was driving a red 1985 Ford pickup that belongs to the Park.

We looked at a mounted buffalo head in the headquarters that measured 17 inches long.

Fred ate lunch with us in our trailer.

The bulls here average 850 pounds dressed meat on the rail. They go from 800 pounds to 1100 pounds. After lunch we videotaped Fred at the headquarters, and then went out and looked at many buffalo. We saw 65 bulls, two years old and older. We saw a long horned bull near the Needles area. We saw a very heavy based bull not too far from the

Buffalo Bull

headquarters, and also another good bull in the same area.

Jim videotaped some ewe bighorn sheep. We also saw elk. I saw one mature 6 by 6 bull. Later, we saw whitetail deer, wild turkey, mule deer, antelope, an owl, a golden eagle, and after dark Jim and I saw an old boar raccoon in the road.

It was cloudy all day today and about 20 degrees Fahrenheit. It sprinkled rain this evening. These Black Hills look to me like they might be part glacial moraine.

There are supposed to be 850 buffalo in Custer State Park. Of this number, 60 are supposedly bulls. Each year they kill 10 bulls that are about 10 years old. The permits for this hunt are by drawing. I was an alternate and was called after one of the hunters had a death in his family and couldn't show up for his hunt. There had already been nine other bulls killed by the time I arrived. I was the last one to hunt. Fred said we would be "scraping the bottom of the barrel". Maybe God will smile on me and give me a Boone & Crockett bull anyway. We turned in early, 9:30, as we have a big day planned tomorrow.

January 30, Thursday.

We arose at 7:00 a.m. and had breakfast. Fred met us at our trailer. We went to look for either of the two bulls we had seen and decided to pass up the day before. Next, Fred and I went up to find the big bulls that we had seen in the Needles area yesterday. We found them after we got the truck stuck and made a lot of noise getting the truck out. They had spooked and ran down a little valley. We had to turn around and go back the way we had come. We went around another way and came back into the same canyon further down. The bulls were feeding in a meadow. They bolted and ran up a ridge and we went up into the timber to get a closer look at them. We decided one of them was big enough to shoot.

About this time another ranger yelled at us from the road that he had spotted a bunch of six bulls high up in a meadow near the Eagles Nest area. Wanting to be sure we got the biggest bull, Fred and I decided to go take a look at them. The road had deep snow on it and was slick with a steep drop off. We made it without any trouble. There was a large bull with them, about 10 years old. The bull looked old with wide flaring horns and lighter coat. I decided to pass him up and go back to the Needles area for the other bull we had seen there.

When we got to the meadow near where we had seen the other two big bulls, there was another single bull feeding across the meadow near the mouth of the small canyon where the first two bulls had come from. We quickly determined that he was a different buffalo than the other two that had been spotted there earlier. We looked at him very closely in the spotting scope and tried to judge his horns. Then Fred, Jim, and I climbed the ridge and located the other two bulls. I studied them in the spotting scope and decided that the bull in the meadow had the larger horns and was probably older. He was the one I should shoot. I sneaked as close as I thought possible without scaring him and took a prone shooting position. I waited until his head was turned slightly away and shot him from a back angle into the brain. He dropped dead in his tracks and never quivered. The 180 grain 30.06 bullet did it's work well. Time of kill was 12:22 p.m.

His head and coat are dark black with a tawny yellow on his

shoulders. He is a beautiful bull. His hide has no rub spots at all. His horns are 19 inches long. After a 60 day drying period, the horns scored 117 Boone & Crockett points. He will go into the top one-third of Safari Club International Record Book.

This hunt was exciting because the buffalo in Custer State Park are wild and roam over a vast and rugged area of 100,000 acres. Even though I was the last one of ten to hunt, I succeeded in taking one of the largest bulls killed that year.

Chapter 29

DON'T BREAK ANY LAWS!!

Most everyone who has ever hunted or fished has at some time, broken a law, some purposely, most accidentally or inadvertently. Ego and greed cause people to break laws on purpose. Others have shot an illegal hen pheasant as it flew toward the sun, making it look redder and mistaking it for a rooster. Still others, in the excitement of the moment failed to immediately tag a game animal or have caught one too many fish.

If you have poached or broken laws, don't tell people about it or brag, but make a resolution to never break anymore laws. You can't change the past, but you can change the future.

Don't shoot after or before legal shooting time, not even a minute. Make sure your watch is accurate.

Don't shoot from a roadway, no matter how big the trophy is.

Never shoot any farther than you are confident of a clean kill.

Never, absolutely never, shoot at anything that you have not positively identified as a legal game animal or bird.

Never litter. Never! Never! If you see litter, pick it up. Take license numbers and turn in people who do litter. Keep our hunting areas clean.

Don't waste game meat. If you don't want it, give it to a needy family or other needy organization.

Don't shoot animals on someone else's license. Shoot only your own and be happy with what you get.

Don't be a slob hunter. Set a good example for other people. It is contagious.

We have to clean up our sport, each one of us personally or the anti-hunters will use our own example to take our sport from us.

Bill Butler, 1992

MONTANA FISH, WILDLIFE, AND PARKS DECOY PROGRAM

Life has gotten tougher for those individuals who would shoot at game out-of-season or after legal hunting hours, shoot from roads, shoot from a vehicle and other wildlife-related violations of Montana law.

A new provision in Montana's hunting statutes makes it illegal to shoot at, or attempt to shoot at, wildlife decoys or other facsimiles of deer, elk and other wildlife species used by the Department of Fish, Wildlife and Parks for enforcement purposes. The enactment of this law, which was passed by the 1991 Legislature and took effect on July 1 of 1991, gives state game wardens an important new means to prevent poachers from

207

stealing wildlife from the public. The new decoy program also provides wardens with an avenue for responding to recurring landowner concerns about shooting before or after legal hunting hours, shooting near buildings and hunting without permission.

Although decoys have been used to deter poachers in other states for several years, Montana law, prior to the passage of Senate Bill 291, did not include a provision that makes it illegal to shoot at facsimiles of wildlife. Many other states still have not enacted a similar law and the absence of such a provision has sometimes hampered prosecution of those who, by all outward appearances, were intent on illegally taking wildlife. FW&P officials hope the new law will not only help curtail illegal activities, but also increase the agency's effectiveness in apprehending those who would illegally kill wildlife and bringing them to justice.

The penalty for attempting to take a wildlife decoy is the same as prescribed for unlawfully taking the wildlife species simulated. As such, those caught shooting at, or attempting to shoot at, a decoy face sizeable fines and possible loss of hunting privileges.

Yet, the real value of any decoy program lies in its deterrent effect and the fact that our valuable wildlife resources do not have to be compromised for those who break the law to be prosecuted. Department officials hope that by informing the public of the existence of the decoy enforcement program, many would-be poachers will reconsider the wisdom of their ways.

Who knows? Those telltale eyes staring spellbound into the glare of a poacher's spotlight may be the real thing, or they may have been manufactured in Cleveland.

POACHER HOTLINE

Poachers are just about as unpopular in Montana as locusts on ripe wheat. TIP-MONT, the Montana Department of Fish, Wildlife and Parks' toll free "Turn in Poachers, Montana," hotline celebrates its eighth anniversary in 1993. The program is sportsman-financed. The money to fund it comes out of the general license revenue. And the calls that come in are primarily from sportsmen themselves.

The Montana Legislature passed the TIP-MONT program in 1985, allowing FW&P to set up and operate the 24-hour toll-free hotline.

Calls have led to the arrest and conviction of deer, bear, elk, moose, and upland game bird poachers. The department averages ten calls per week. Callers may remain anonymous and do not have to testify in court.

The number is 1-800-TIP-MONT (1-800-847-6668).